W9-AXQ-647

Round

AND

Round

TOGETHER

Round

AND

Round

TOGETHER

*Taking a Merry-Go-Round Ride
into the Civil Rights Movement*

AMY NATHAN

PAUL DRY BOOKS
Philadelphia   2011

Cover photos

Top: Daniel Conry and Jhade Carney riding the Carousel on the Mall, located on the National Mall in Washington, D.C., where it has been since 1981. Back in 1963, this merry-go-round was at Baltimore's Gwynn Oak Amusement Park, the site of civil rights protests from 1955 to 1963. Photo © James Singewald. *Bottom:* Eleven-month-old Sharon Langley and her father, Charles C. Langley, Jr., on the merry-go-round when it was still at Gwynn Oak Amusement Park on August 28, 1963, the day the park integrated. Photo Courtesy Baltimore Sun Company, Inc., All Rights Reserved.

Frontispiece photos

Background: The Carousel on the Mall. *Foreground:* Two white youngsters rode on either side of Sharon Langley during her first merry-go-round ride at Gwynn Oak. Photo Courtesy Baltimore Sun Company, Inc., All Rights Reserved.

For a full list of photo and text permissions, see page 246, which constitutes an extension of this copyright page.

First Paul Dry Books Edition, 2011

Paul Dry Books, Inc.
Philadelphia, Pennsylvania
www.pauldrybooks.com

Copyright © 2011 Amy Nathan
All rights reserved
www.AmyNathanBooks.com

Typefaces: Calluna, Scala Sans, Metroscript, and Frutiger
Designed and composed by P. M. Gordon Associates

Printed in the United States of America

Library of Congress Cataloging-in-Publication Data

Nathan, Amy.
  Round and round together : a merry-go-round's spot in the civil rights
movement / Amy Nathan. — 1st Paul Dry Books ed.
      p. cm.
  Includes bibliographical references and index.
  ISBN 978-1-58988-071-9 (alk. paper)
    1. African Americans—Civil rights—Maryland—Baltimore—History—20th
century—Juvenile literature. 2. Civil rights movements—Maryland—Baltimore—
History—20th century—Juvenile literature. 3. Baltimore (Md.)—Race relations—
Juvenile literature. 4. Gwynn Oak (Baltimore, Md.)—Race relations—Juvenile
literature. 5. Gwynn Oak Park (Baltimore, Md.)—History—Juvenile literature.
6. African Americans—Civil rights—Maryland—Baltimore—Biography—Juvenile
literature. l. Title.
  F189.B19N458 2011
  323.1196'07307526—dc23

                                                            2011029073

*To all who had the courage
to stand up
and speak out*

Contents

Round

AND

Round

TOGETHER

"Gwynn Oak stood out as a symbol of all the evils inherent in the system of segregation. . . . It was a symbol that had to be faced and challenged."

—Rev. Frank Williams, Letter to the Editor,
The Sun, August 22, 1963

Courtesy Baltimore Sun

A SPECIAL RIDE

A HIGHLIGHT OF MANY VISITS to the National Mall in Washington, D.C., is having a chance to climb aboard a classic, old-time merry-go-round. What a treat for kids and adults alike to settle into the saddle of a handsome wooden horse, grip the reins, and let imaginations wander as the horse glides up and down, circling round and round, while jingling music fills the air.

In addition to being a beauty, this merry-go-round is part of history—not just because it's more than sixty years old and sits in front of the headquarters of the Smithsonian Institution, the world's largest museum complex.

This merry-go-round gained its spot in history because of a little girl in a pink dress and the ride she took on one of its dappled horses on August 28, 1963. On that hot summer day, the merry-go-round had not yet taken up its position on the National Mall. It was still part of Gwynn Oak Amusement Park, located about forty miles away on the outskirts of Baltimore, Maryland.

Sharon Langley, the history-making young rider, was a month shy of her first birthday when her parents took her to Gwynn Oak Park that Wednesday. Newspaper reporters swarmed around the

Facing page: Sharon Langley with her father, Charles C. Langley, Jr., on the merry-go-round at Gwynn Oak Amusement Park, August 28, 1963.

family, asking questions and snapping photos of Sharon's historic ride. The next day, newspapers in several cities across the nation reported on her amusement park visit.

What was so history-making about a little girl riding a merry-go-round? The fact that she and her family were able to enter the park at all, without being harassed, beaten, or arrested. For nearly seventy years, Gwynn Oak's owners had kept African American families like the Langleys out of the park. Black youngsters weren't allowed to ride on the merry-go-round or on any of the park's other attractions. A whites-only policy of racial segregation had been the rule.

On August 28, 1963, the park finally changed its rules, as a result of nearly ten years of protests. For the first time, African Americans were able to enter the park and buy tickets, just like everyone else.

Sharon Langley was the first black child to go on a ride there that day. Her father stood next to her, keeping a firm grip on his young daughter so she wouldn't slip out of the saddle. On either side of Sharon was a white youngster. As the merry-go-round's creaky wooden platform picked up speed, skin tones blended in a blur of happy faces. A gentle breeze fluttered the frilly collar on Sharon's dress. Three kids—one black and two white—each perched on a beautiful horse, were sitting side by side, going up and down, round and round, having fun together.

It's a scene that would have brought a smile to the face of a man who was busy that day making history himself about an hour's drive away in Washington, D.C.—the Rev. Dr. Martin Luther King, Jr. This was the day Dr. King gave his famous "I Have a Dream" speech in front of hundreds of thousands of people gathered near the National Mall for the March on Washington for Jobs and Freedom. Dr. King spoke about his dream that one day African American children would no longer be treated unfairly because of the color of their skin, that all kids—white and black—would treat each other as sisters and brothers.

Sharon Langley's merry-go-round ride gave hope that Dr. King's dream might come true. If kids could learn to have fun together at

Two white youngsters rode on either side of Sharon Langley during her first merry-go-round ride at Gwynn Oak.

Courtesy Baltimore Sun

this park, the scene of turmoil for so many years, then maybe people could learn to get along elsewhere, too.

A HOPE—AND A WARNING

There were no riots at Gwynn Oak as Sharon rode on her merry-go-round horse that day, nor were there any in the weeks to come. Letting reality live up to the ideals set forth in the Declaration of Independence turned out not to be impossible or as scary as some had feared. One hundred years after the Emancipation Proclamation ended slavery during the Civil War, the country was beginning to fulfill the promise of freedom for all.

However, that little girl's merry-go-round ride also warned that making Dr. King's dream come true everywhere would be difficult indeed. Changing just this one amusement park took nearly ten years of protests. Summer after summer, from 1955 to 1963, protestors tried to end segregation there. They walked picket lines, carried signs, wrote letters, tried to reason with the park's owners, and sometimes were assaulted and arrested.

The citizens—both black and white—who demonstrated at Gwynn Oak during those years included college students, teachers, professors, social workers, housewives, union members, lawyers, religious leaders, community organizers, journalists, teenagers, elementary school kids, and even some politicians. One family that played a key role traced its ancestry back to both an African chief and a slave-owning signer of the Declaration of Independence. These varied participants showed that it takes more than a famous leader to make history and bring about change. Also essential are many so-called "ordinary" people, who prove by their courage and commitment that they're not ordinary after all. These dedicated individuals were determined to keep protesting until every child had the right to ride that beautiful merry-go-round—even though it took nearly a decade.

CHANGING MINDS

"When you look back at it, it's rather silly that it took so long. Things were set in people's minds. Segregation is the way it had always been and people came to believe that's the way it's got to be. If we had just let all our kids go there and play, they would have been playing together without thinking about race at all," said Charles Mason. He was 25 years old in 1963, fresh out of Baltimore's largely black Morgan State College (now Morgan State University). That summer, this young activist helped organize demonstrations at Gwynn Oak that were much larger and far more effective than protests in previous years. The dramatic demonstrations he helped plan for 1963 succeeded—finally—in opening up the park to all.

That summer's protests featured bold new tactics that hadn't been directed at the park before. Over the years, Baltimoreans had tried a variety of strategies at Gwynn Oak. The changing menu of methods provides a good illustration of the evolving tactical lineup being used during those years by the civil rights movement as a whole.

© Bob Adelman/Corbis

Rev. Dr. Martin Luther King, Jr., giving his "I Have a Dream" speech, August 28, 1963, at the March on Washington for Jobs and Freedom.

The Gwynn Oak campaign spanned an important period in civil rights history—from 1955 to 1963—beginning a few months before Dr. King made his first appearance on the protest scene and ending the same summer as his monumental March on Washington.

During those nine years, Baltimore activists sometimes found themselves ahead of the curve in trying new strategies. At other times, Baltimoreans adopted tactics that had proved successful elsewhere in the country. Baltimore protestors were dedicated volunteers who learned gradually along the way what worked—and what didn't—in their quest to bring a peaceful end to an unjust social system. They allied themselves with various civil rights organizations, groups that competed and disagreed with each other at times but pulled together at important moments, putting differences aside to achieve their common goal. It was the same kind of on-the-job learning that civil rights activists around the country experienced. They all were searching for just the right combination of tactics to exert enough pressure on people to persuade them to have the courage to do the right thing and end segregation.

Figuring out which strategies worked was a dynamic, changing process, spurred forward in the final years by the impatient energy of young people such as Charles Mason, who was fed up with waiting for things to improve. Some who participated in the climactic 1963 demonstrations at Gwynn Oak were a good deal younger than Mr. Mason, including two little boys, ages six and eight, who were hauled off in a police car with their parents and baby brother. An 11-year-old girl helped that summer, too, by going on an undercover mission at the park with her aunt. Photos and stories about these kids appeared in newspapers and played a role in bringing an end to the park's unfair rules, showing that regular folks, kids included, can make a difference.

"IT WAS SYMBOLIC"

It may seem puzzling that so many people spent so much time and energy trying to open up an amusement park when there were more serious problems of discrimination in the areas of education, jobs, and housing. Baltimore activists were working hard on those issues, too. But a park that kept toddlers from riding a merry-go-round just because of skin tone seemed so obviously unfair that it stood out as a symbol of a whole system of discrimination that needed to change. "Gwynn Oak was the mountaintop of the Baltimore civil rights demonstrations," said Judge Robert Watts. This Morgan graduate was a young lawyer in 1963, offering his services for free to hundreds of protestors arrested in the final demonstrations that ended segregation at Gwynn Oak.

"It was symbolic, as so many things were," explained Robert Bell, who became chief judge of the Maryland Court of Appeals

WHY AMUSEMENT PARKS

About four months before the August 1963 March on Washington, Rev. Dr. Martin Luther King, Jr., was arrested during demonstrations in Birmingham, Alabama. While in jail, he wrote a letter (published later) in which he explained why he protested. One of his reasons: "When you suddenly find your tongue twisted and your speech stammering as you seek to explain to your six-year-old daughter why she can't go to the amusement park that has just been advertised on television, and see tears welling up in her little eyes when she is told that Funtown is closed to colored children, and see the depressing clouds of inferiority begin to form in her little mental sky . . . then you will understand why we find it difficult to wait."

in 1996. He was arrested as a teenager in 1960 for trying to integrate a Baltimore restaurant. "Who cares whether you could go, other than the fact that you can. It's symbolic. You choose your battles and go with those things that have the least reason to be challenged. If you can get those out of the way, then you can move more easily to go after the bigger things."

Gwynn Oak had a special importance to Baltimore activists because neighborhoods near the park were becoming increasingly African American. "A lot of the kids who lived in that area wanted to know why they couldn't go there," said Marie Williams, who, as a 20-year-old, helped sign up demonstrators for the 1963 protests. "I didn't care that I couldn't go to Gwynn Oak, because I wasn't an amusement park person. I didn't like being way up in the air and being dropped down. I picketed and did all this for someone else, for later on down the years."

"I'm not sure that it was not being able to go to an amusement park that was so offensive as not having the *right* to go if I wanted to," added Mary Sue Welcome, a 19-year-old Gwynn Oak protestor in 1963. By 2010, she had become one of Maryland's assistant attorneys general. "I was doing my part, trying to make things better in my little corner of the world."

LIVING HISTORY

The Gwynn Oak victory was just one among many in the long struggle to end segregation. However, it left behind a concrete symbol that can remind people of the many small steps that had to be taken in order to create a more just society: the merry-go-round ridden by an African American youngster on August 28, 1963.

This merry-go-round made its way to the National Mall because of a hurricane that damaged Gwynn Oak Amusement Park so severely that the park closed permanently. However, the merry-go-round weathered the storm. A company that runs concession stands at the Smithsonian bought it. In 1981, it moved to Washington's National Mall to a prime spot right in front of the Smithsonian's Arts and Industries Building.

Renamed the Carousel on the Mall, it has given rides for decades to thousands of kids—and grown-ups, too—who visit Washington, people of all races, religions, and nationalities. A short stroll away is the Lincoln Memorial, on whose steps Dr. King stood in August 1963 to deliver his famous speech.

The Smithsonian concessionaire didn't choose Gwynn Oak's merry-go-round because of its role in the civil rights movement. He chose it because it was a large, sturdy example of a classic carousel (the French name for a merry-go-round). But knowing about the merry-go-round's history adds a special meaning to climbing onboard. Riding round and round on it can serve as a reminder of a little girl's 1963 ride, which offered a sweetly hope-filled promise of Dr. King's dream brought to life, a symbol of the harmony he sought.

A ride on this merry-go-round can also illustrate the long struggle that led to its liberation. A merry-go-round circles its riders round and round without getting them anywhere, depositing them back where they started. For many years, protesting at

Since 1981, the National Mall in Washington, D.C., has been home to the merry-go-round that Sharon Langley rode at Gwynn Oak in 1963.

© James Singewald

TERMINOLOGY

"We have evolved from colored to Negro, to blacks, to African Americans," said Rev. Marion C. Bascom, a civil rights activist in Baltimore during the 1960s, commenting in 2006 on the changing names used over the years for Americans of African ancestry. "Colored" was common in the early 1900s, even finding its way into the name of the NAACP (founded in 1909)—National Association for the Advancement of Colored People. "Negro" was in use in the 1940s when the United Negro College Fund started. However, those two terms fell out of favor during the 1960s, replaced by "black" and "African American," which are the ones used in this book, except for direct quotes from people speaking or writing in earlier years.

Gwynn Oak must have felt like riding a merry-go-round, going round and round without coming any closer to ending segregation. And yet, an idea for a different way forward emerged from the protestors' persistence, leading to victory at last.

In its new life on the National Mall, this merry-go-round shows how far the country has come, as visitors of different backgrounds and ages share a fun experience together, while strains of "The Stars and Stripes Forever" fill the air, providing a sense of hope for a troubled world, not unlike the hope for a better future that kept Gwynn Oak protestors going.

TELLING THE TALE

This book tells the tale of the nearly decade-long struggle to liberate that once whites-only merry-go-round, weaving its story into that of the civil rights movement as a whole to show how demonstrations occurring elsewhere influenced the Gwynn Oak protestors.

Understanding what was involved in achieving this one step forward at Gwynn Oak can give a greater appreciation for what the wider civil rights struggle was like. The concerned Baltimoreans who kept trying different tactics and adapting their protest strategies were typical of civil rights volunteers in other cities and towns, all chipping away as best they could until the walls of segregation came crumbling down.

"So we organized this youth movement to get jobs, to fight discrimination and to do something about the problems we were encountering."

—Juanita Jackson Mitchell in the oral history she recorded for Maryland Historical Society, July 25, 1975

© James Singewald

SETTING THE STAGE

THE MERRY-GO-ROUND THAT Sharon Langley rode in August 1963 got its start in 1947, when it arrived brand new at Gwynn Oak Amusement Park, located just outside the northwest corner of Baltimore. Nestled in about sixty-four acres of tree-lined lawns and grassy fields, Gwynn Oak was the oldest and most popular amusement park in the area, the one where families came to picnic and relax, where schools held parties and proms.

Gwynn Oak opened in 1894. It was a Trolley Park, so named because in its early years most people came to the park on streetcars, also called trolleys. Like the hundreds of other Trolley Parks that cropped up around the country during the late 1800s, Gwynn Oak was built by a trolley company whose streetcar line ran past the park. Trolley companies hoped these parks would encourage more people to ride streetcars. By the mid-1920s, Baltimore was a streetcar city, crisscrossed with more than 400 miles of streetcar tracks.

From the start, Gwynn Oak was a whites-only park. The 1890s were a time when segregationist rules and laws took hold in the

Facing page: This photo and those at the start of other chapters show horses on the merry-go-round that Gwynn Oak Amusement Park installed in 1947 and that moved to the National Mall in 1981.

southern region of the United States. A segregated amusement park was just one part of a society that placed many restrictions on African Americans.

Baltimore originally had several Trolley Parks, but the tough times created by the Great Depression of the 1930s, combined with the growing popularity of automobiles, caused streetcar lines to lose riders and Trolley Parks to lose customers. Some of Baltimore's Trolley Parks closed. Not Gwynn Oak.

In 1936, Arthur B. Price, Sr., an ambitious Baltimore businessman who had owned movie theaters in the city and would later be elected president of the Baltimore City Council, took over Gwynn Oak Amusement Park. At first he leased the park from the streetcar company that owned it. He fixed it up, improved its rides, and brought in new attractions, including Bo-Bo the Clown to entertain little kids. During the summer of 1942, a sound truck roamed the streets of Baltimore, blaring out ads for this segregated funspot, no doubt a painful message for the area's African Americans. Mr. Price's improvements paid off. That summer, at the height of World War II, Gwynn Oak reported its best money-making season ever. Before the war ended, Mr. Price bought the park.

World War II actually helped Baltimore's economy, partly explaining Gwynn Oak's success during the 1940s. The city's steel mills, shipyards, and factories were busy around the clock turning out airplanes, ships, weapons, and other equipment for the war. Workers came to Baltimore from other parts of the country to do this war work. Streetcars became popular again, thanks to wartime gas-rationing, which made taking the streetcar to work—or to Gwynn Oak—less of a hassle than trying to gas up a car. Gwynn Oak did so well over the next few years that Mr. Price bought a new merry-go-round in 1947.

Gwynn Oak, like other Trolley Parks, was in a country setting, offering city dwellers a break from urban bustle. A stream ran through the park. There were picnic areas, tennis courts, and a baseball field, as well as a lake with boats for rent. The park offered band concerts, circus acts, pony and goat-cart rides, Fourth of July fireworks, a shooting gallery, a game arcade, and a pavilion where

A trolley brings customers to Gwynn Oak Amusement Park, early twentieth century.

couples could dance to the big band music of local groups or of Glenn Miller and other visiting bands. Food stands sold hot dogs, lemonade, popcorn, and that sticky summertime favorite, cotton candy.

"It was magnificent," said Alison Turaj Brown. As a white youngster growing up in a Baltimore suburb during the 1940s, she visited Gwynn Oak when she was too young to realize there weren't any black kids on the rides with her. In 1963, when she was 25 and had long since become aware of the unfairness of segregation, she was injured protesting against segregation at Gwynn Oak. "I became upset with Baltimore for a while but that didn't kill the good memories," she said. She remembers the fun of riding the trolley to the park as a little girl. "There were coupons for discounts at Gwynn Oak on the ends of bags of bread. The Ferris wheel was my favorite. I remember going on the merry-go-round, but I didn't like the rickety roller coaster. It seemed terribly unsafe."

Unlike today's big theme parks, Trolley Parks didn't charge an entrance fee. People could come in for free, have a picnic, and then,

*Images from Gwynn Oak
Amusement Park in the 1940s.*

if they wished, buy tickets for the rides. There were plenty of rides
to choose among at Gwynn Oak: a Ferris wheel, two wooden roller
coasters—the Big and Little Dipper—bumper cars, a spinning-car
ride called The Whip, and, of course, the merry-go-round.

NEW RIDE—OLD RULES

Over the years, Gwynn Oak had a succession of different merry-
go-rounds. The new one that arrived in 1947 was built by one of
the most famous carousel manufacturers in the country, the Allan

Herschell Company. Its founder, Allan Herschell, a Scottish immigrant, built his first merry-go-round in 1883, about ten years before Gwynn Oak opened. Early Herschell carousel horses were made of wood, hand-carved and hand-painted. By the 1930s, the company was using less-expensive, lighter-weight aluminum for heads and tails. In the 1950s, it switched to all-aluminum horses.

The horses on Gwynn Oak's 1947 ride have hand-carved wooden bodies, with aluminum heads, legs, and tails. They're "jumpers," with all four feet off the ground. Their racing feet, open mouths, and flowing manes, combined with the daring glint in their eyes, make them seem ready to gallop off at high speed. Their colors range from shocking turquoise to more horse-like shades of white, black, brown, golden palomino, and dappled gray. Also on the ride is a striped zebra. Saddles feature painted flowers, scroll work, or patriotic stars and stripes. In addition, there are wooden chariots with benches for those who prefer not to saddle up. Glittery mirrors and twinkling lights add to the fun, as does the ride's lively music. Originally, the music came from a band organ, which works like a player piano: Paper rolls dotted with perforated holes trigger music-producing pipes and drums.

The year 1947 was a good year for Gwynn Oak to introduce a special new merry-go-round. People were in a mood to celebrate. World War II had just ended and soldiers had returned home, eager to spend time with their families.

But for returning African American soldiers, there would be no kicking back and relaxing at Gwynn Oak, no merry-go-round rides for their kids. Gwynn Oak was still whites-only.

"Segregated parks were widespread back then, although there were some parks that were always open to everyone and a few that were just for blacks," said Jim Abbate of the National Amusement Park Historical Association. "At some of the old, traditional segregated parks, they'd be open one day a season for blacks." From the mid-1950s to 1970s, Maryland had a black-owned park, Carr's Beach Amusement Park, about an hour's drive south of Baltimore. When this park first opened, Carr's Beach was one of the few beaches in that part of Maryland that blacks could use.

Whites-only amusement parks were common not only in Southern states, but also in states like Maryland on the northern rim of the South. Segregated parks could also be found in states farther north. Until 1949, New Jersey's Palisades Amusement Park allowed African Americans on the park's rides but not in the park's swimming pool. In Ohio, Cincinnati's Coney Island Park was totally off limits to blacks until protestors forced it to change in 1955, but its pool remained whites-only for another six years. In Washington state, Spokane's Natatorium amusement park kept blacks out of its pool during the 1940s and also out of its dance pavilion whenever white musicians were performing. However, if black musicians were playing, African Americans were welcome to come spend their money and dance.

In Michigan, it took a 1948 U.S. Supreme Court ruling to end discrimination on the steamships that took people to an amusement park on Bob-Lo Island, located about fifteen miles from Detroit in the Detroit River. Before then, steamships owned by the company that ran the park claimed the right to refuse to carry black passengers. One of those excluded from the ship was Sarah Ray, a young woman who, in 1945, filed an official complaint, which led to the Supreme Court case.

THE WAY IT WAS

Of course, segregation in the 1940s affected more than amusement parks. Throughout the South there were laws designed to keep blacks and whites from having much to do with each other. Some laws prevented African Americans from sitting in the same section of a bus or train as white people. Other laws kept blacks from going to schools, hospitals, and libraries with whites, or from using the same water fountains and restrooms. Marriage between blacks and whites was also forbidden.

Many Southern businesses set their own discriminatory rules, extending segregation's reach. Southern movie theaters often made blacks sit in the balcony instead of downstairs in the better

From the Jim Crow South, a segregated waiting room in a North Carolina bus station, 1940.

seats. Most Southern restaurants kept out blacks. Even churches were often segregated. Some businesses in Northern states also had discriminatory rules. In the 1940s there were whites-only restaurants in such Northern cities as Chicago, Syracuse, and Denver.

Not only were these laws and rules offensive to African Americans, so was the collective name given to them: Jim Crow. This insulting term for blacks originated before the Civil War, popularized in the 1830s by white minstrel show performers. They would blacken their faces with burnt cork and strut about the stage doing crude impersonations of enslaved African Americans, singing a song called "Jump Jim Crow."

By the end of the Civil War in 1865, slavery had ended in the United States, but many white Southerners refused to give up the old ways of thinking. Less than fifteen years later, segregationists had managed to gain control of state governments down South.

Before long, their legislatures began passing discriminatory laws nicknamed for that minstrel show caricature, Jim Crow.

STAMP OF APPROVAL

Blacks protested Jim Crow laws but were unable to stop their spread, especially after the U.S. Supreme Court gave its stamp of approval in 1896, two years after Gwynn Oak Amusement Park opened. The Supreme Court's ruling in a case called *Plessy v. Ferguson* led to an avalanche of new Jim Crow laws throughout the South. That 1896 court case involved a new law the Louisiana legislature passed in 1890. It said that blacks and whites could no longer do what they had been doing for many years—sit together in the same train cars. Louisiana citizens who opposed this law formed a group called the Citizens Committee. They decided to challenge the law by having an African American arrested for sitting in a whites-only car. Homer Plessy, a New Orleans shoemaker, volunteered to be arrested. His skin was so light in color that it was easy for him to enter a train car for whites. When he announced that he was black, he was taken off to jail.

The Citizens Committee thought a judge would realize the law was unfair and overturn Homer Plessy's arrest. Instead, John Ferguson, a Louisiana judge, ruled that it was perfectly all right for the police to have arrested Mr. Plessy. The Citizens Committee hired lawyers to appeal that ruling all the way to the U.S. Supreme Court. They were stunned when it decided in 1896 that there was nothing wrong with Louisiana's train law. The Supreme Court ruled that segregation was acceptable because the law said that blacks would be provided with separate-but-equal facilities. This separate-but-equal idea would be used for many years to justify the existence of the whole Jim Crow system.

But the separate facilities that were provided for blacks—whether in a train, bus, library, hospital, or school—were never truly equal to the higher quality services available for whites. It would be nearly sixty years, however, before the Supreme Court acknowledged the sham of separate-but-equal and took a forceful stand against Jim Crow. Until then, some brave individuals in various Southern states continued to protest. For many years those efforts met with limited success. Most people simply struggled to find ways to cope with this unnatural way of living. In the South, speaking up against Jim Crow was risky. It could get a person beaten, arrested, or even killed.

Among the most effective laws for solidifying the Jim Crow system were those that set up a variety of complex tests, rules, and unfair taxes that made it almost impossible for African Americans in the South to register and vote. So it is not at all surprising that segregationists kept being elected to run Southern state governments.

JIM CROW IN MARYLAND

When that new merry-go-round arrived at Gwynn Oak in 1947, Maryland had several Jim Crow laws on the books, including ones that kept its schools segregated and made interracial marriage illegal. (The marriage restriction wasn't lifted until 1967.) Also segregated during the 1940s were Baltimore's playgrounds, public parks, swimming pools, and other recreational facilities. Blacks in Baltimore couldn't be firefighters, taxicab drivers, or city bus drivers. In general, job opportunities for Maryland's African American citizens were very limited. Businesses that hired blacks tended to place them in lower-paid jobs. The police department hired its first black officers in 1937, but until the early 1940s those officers couldn't wear regular police uniforms, "because white people would not stand for black officers arresting them," noted Juanita Jackson Mitchell, a lawyer who would defend protestors arrested in 1963 at Gwynn Oak.

Many businesses in Maryland established their own Jim Crow rules. In the 1940s and 1950s, these rules limited African American access to many of Maryland's restaurants, hotels, theaters, department stores, beauty shops, hospitals, nursing homes, bowling alleys, swimming pools, beaches—and amusement parks. Judge Robert Watts recalled what it was like when he started out as a

JIM CROW RIP OFF

T. D. Rice, the white entertainer who made "Jump Jim Crow" a hit tune in the 1830s, may have gotten his ideas from African American dancers he saw at a New York City market. It was a popular spot where black farm workers sold produce and held dance contests, performing dances and songs from their African past. Before 1827, when slavery ended in New York, many of the dancers would have been enslaved. African folklore often features a trickster animal—sometimes a crow—who outsmarts the powerful. Mr. Rice is said to have learned to dance by watching those dancers and may have picked up from them the idea for "Jump Jim Crow." Blackening his face with burnt cork and advertising himself as the "original Jim Crow," he entertained mostly white audiences with exaggerated portrayals of a raunchy Jim Crow, who tricked slave masters. His caricatured creation, a distortion of African culture, later became attached to laws that oppressed the descendants of that culture.

young lawyer in Baltimore in 1950. If he was downtown working on a case with white lawyers, sometimes those lawyers would suggest going out for a cup of coffee, forgetting that this was impossible for him. "I couldn't go in and sit down at the lunch counter," he explained. Instead a white friend would go to a nearby grocery store and buy food for Mr. Watts so this future judge could "sit out on the steps and eat my lunch."

Jim Crow rules could trip up white youngsters, too, as happened with Alison Turaj Brown in the late 1940s. "As a child, you didn't know about segregation until you did something wrong—drank at the wrong water fountain, sat in the wrong seat. When I was about 11, I became aware of segregation when I sat down in the wrong section of a trolley and was told to get up," said Ms. Brown. During her childhood, she spent summers in Connecticut where "you sat wherever you wanted on a bus or trolley." Back home in Maryland, she rode a trolley to school. Although historians report that Baltimore-area streetcars were not officially segregated, individual conductors and passengers might enforce their own seating preferences. One day, on her way home from school, young Alison took a seat toward the back of the trolley, with the black passengers. The conductor told her to move toward the front, with the whites. She refused. "I remember being put off the trolley. It was a shock. I had to walk quite a way to get home. Then my parents explained everything to me. My parents were proud of me. They told me I had done the right thing." Her family had a long history of being in favor of equal rights. In the early 1900s, her grandfather had been part of an organization that led to the creation in 1909 of a leading civil rights group, the NAACP (National Association for the Advancement of Colored People).

Some stores' Jim Crow rules were especially offensive. For many years, Baltimore's big downtown department stores refused to let African Americans buy clothes. That changed in the 1950s, but the stores still placed insulting restrictions on black shoppers. They weren't allowed to try on clothes in the stores. Nor could they return the clothes later. Blacks were also excluded from department store restaurants and from having charge accounts. Black families who could afford to take day trips north to Pennsylvania often preferred shopping in Philadelphia, where stores didn't practice that kind of discrimination.

"Young people today can't understand how things could have been the way they were, how there could be a time when you couldn't go downtown and try on clothes," noted Charles Mason, an organizer of the 1963 Gwynn Oak protests. Assistant Attorney General Mary Sue Welcome recalled that as a teenager in the 1950s she initiated a spur-of-the-moment personal protest against the department store rule "that you couldn't try on their hats." She and a girlfriend went into one of the downtown stores and purposely tried on hats until a salesperson stopped them. "When I got home and told my mother what I had done, she didn't like me going off on my own doing that kind of thing. But I was making a statement, going through the indignity of not being able to try on hats, striking a blow."

MARYLAND IN THE MIDDLE

It's not surprising that Maryland had restrictive Jim Crow rules and laws, given its history as a major slave-owning state. In many ways, Maryland has much in common with other former slave states farther south. The name of Gwynn Oak Amusement Park's dance pavilion—the Dixie Ballroom—shows Maryland's Southern leanings.

Maryland's history regarding race is complex and often contradictory. In the Civil War, Maryland never joined the eleven Southern slave states in the Confederacy that were at war with the rest of the nation. Even so, during most of the war years, Maryland citizens were allowed to continue to enslave African Americans. That was because of Maryland's special status as one of five Border States. Northern leaders permitted slavery in the Border States to help keep them from joining the Confederacy.

Also surprising, enslaved people in Maryland weren't actually freed by President Abraham Lincoln's 1863 Emancipation Proclamation. It ended slavery *only* in states that had joined the Confederacy, not in the Border States. Emancipation arrived in Maryland a year later, in 1864, when Maryland changed its state constitution to outlaw slavery.

Adding to the complexity, besides having thousands of enslaved people before the Civil War, Maryland also had a large population of African Americans who were free. In 1860, on the eve of the Civil War, nearly half the state's blacks were free. However, life for these free blacks was harsh, with limited educational and employment opportunities. Before the Civil War, Maryland was also home to an active group of abolitionists who called for an end to slavery. But when William Lloyd Garrison, a Northern abolitionist, gave an anti-slavery speech in Baltimore in 1830, he was arrested and run out of town.

After the Civil War, a strong African American community developed in Baltimore, made stronger during the twentieth century by a huge influx of blacks from states farther south, hoping for more freedom and opportunity. Between 1930 and 1950, Baltimore's black population increased by about sixty percent.

"My parents grew up in Virginia and used to tell me about lynchings they had seen there," recalled Charles Mason. His parents left Virginia in the 1940s after yet another of these mob-incited hangings of a black man. They decided Baltimore might be a safer place to raise Charles and his sister. "Baltimore was supposed to be a Northern city, but it was still a Southern city in mood and atmosphere, although none of those really brutal incidents happened here," he said. Lynchings took place in Maryland in earlier years, but none occurred there after 1933.

One aspect of Jim Crow actually helped Baltimore's African Americans develop a strong sense of community. Housing was segregated in Baltimore, with a complex web of regulations, contracts, and informal rules that for many years prevented blacks from moving into certain sections of the city. From the 1930s through 1950s, most African Americans lived in a mile-square area in the northwestern section of the inner city. There were also smaller all-black neighborhoods in parts of East and South Baltimore. "We had our own neighborhoods that were pretty much self-contained," noted Judge Robert Bell, who grew up in Baltimore in the 1950s. There wasn't much need for him and other black youngsters to venture out of those neighborhoods. They attended segregated neighborhood schools and played in local parks. "We had our own shopping area and segregated movie theaters. My mother was from the South and had seen all the mistreatment there. There was a concerted effort on the part of our parents to protect us from those kinds of things. We never had a chance to see the separate restrooms and water fountains unless we went downtown," he explained.

"But I did see it in the summer when I went south to visit my relatives in North Carolina," he noted. "It was starkly realistic down there. If you went south on the bus, once you left Washington, D.C., you switched seats to the back of the bus. If you went to buy a barbecue sandwich, you went to the back door to buy it.

They'd allow you to take it out but wouldn't allow you to walk into the restaurant. If you went to a store, you'd have to wait until somebody else was waited on if the other person was white. I saw that and knew all about that. I saw the superiority exerted over my relatives, and I saw the way that they accepted it. That was never something that I thought was appropriate. But it was something you didn't see every day in Baltimore unless you went downtown."

Something else different about Maryland: It never enacted the severe kinds of laws that kept blacks from being able to vote, as many Southern states did, although some Maryland segregationists tried hard to pass such laws in the early 1900s. For much of the twentieth century, African Americans in Maryland generally were able to register and vote. This gap in Maryland's Jim Crow system played a major role in eventually bringing the system to an end, when activists realized the importance of marshalling black voting power.

YOUTH POWER

During the 1930s, Baltimore's tightly-knit African American community began to challenge certain aspects of Jim Crow. The kinds of protest activities that started in those years would have a big impact later in the campaign to end discrimination at Gwynn Oak Amusement Park.

Three types of institutions led this move toward protest in the 1930s. First, some black churches began discussing social and political issues, making their buildings available as meeting places for protest groups and often providing those groups with financial support. Churches would play a similar role years later in the Gwynn Oak struggle.

A black-owned newspaper, the *Baltimore Afro-American*, also played a role in supporting protest. John Murphy, a former slave, had started this newspaper in 1892, shortly before Gwynn Oak Amusement Park opened. After his death in 1922, his son Carl Murphy took over as editor and led the paper until the 1960s. Carl Murphy was a strong voice for change in the black community.

His newspaper kept the community informed with hard-hitting investigative reporting, especially important because until the 1950s the city's major white-owned newspaper, the *Sun*, included little coverage of black events.

The third element in the move toward protest was the appearance of local branches of two national civil rights organizations, the Urban League and the NAACP. Baltimore's Urban League chapter used persuasion and behind-the-scenes negotiations to try to expand educational and job opportunities for African Americans. The NAACP would become known for using more assertive tactics, but in the mid-1930s Baltimore's NAACP chapter wasn't very active. That changed thanks to two energetic African American teenagers, Juanita Jackson and her sister Virginia.

Juanita Jackson Mitchell

Their family history illustrates the complexity of Maryland's relationship with race. Their mother claimed she was descended both from an African chief and from Charles Carroll of Carrollton, a white Maryland slave owner and signer of the Declaration of Independence, on whose plantation the Jackson sisters' grandfather lived.

The activism of these two sisters provides an early example of young people leading the way, something that came into play years later at Gwynn Oak. In 1931, even though Juanita Jackson was only 18 years old, she had just graduated from the University of Pennsylvania in Philadelphia. Her sister Virginia, a 19-year-old artist, had just graduated from the Philadelphia School of Art. Both went to college in Philadelphia because neither the University of Maryland nor art schools in Baltimore would admit black students. The younger sister, Juanita, noted that "interracial living and interracial educational activities" in Philadelphia provided a welcome holiday from Jim Crow. "We could eat anywhere," she said. How discouraging that "just a few miles down the road here was Baltimore so strictly segregated."

When these two college graduates returned home to Baltimore in 1931, they were unable to find jobs. Of course, jobs were scarce for everyone then, the height of the Great Depression. It was especially tough for African Americans, who weren't even allowed to apply for many jobs. A good option for female college graduates back then—becoming a librarian—was off limits to blacks. Teaching in black schools was permitted, but there were no openings in 1931. The younger sister finally found a teaching job the next year and taught at a Baltimore vocational school for two years.

But in 1931, when the Jackson sisters were still unemployed, they organized a youth group, the City-Wide Young People's Forum. They invited other out-of-work African American young people to join them for regular Friday night meetings at a church to discuss how to change Baltimore.

One of their first targets: white-owned businesses that refused to hire African Americans even though the businesses were right in the middle of black neighborhoods. The northwest section of

Baltimore where the Jackson family lived "was a hundred percent black ghetto," said Juanita Jackson Mitchell (the name she
used after she married in 1938). "We couldn't work in the stores.
The stores that sold us all our merchandise would not hire us as
sales people." One young man who came to their meetings suggested boycotting the stores—refusing to shop at the stores until
they hired black workers. If those businesses began to lose money,
maybe they would change their hiring practices. A boycott like
this had been tried a few years earlier in Chicago. The Baltimore
youth group began its boycott in 1933. Their slogan was "Don't Buy
Where You Can't Work."

Courtesy Afro-American Newspapers Archives

*Protestors walk the picket line as part of Baltimore's "Don't Buy Where You
Can't Work" boycott, December 1933.*

Courtesy Afro-American Newspapers Archives

Two clerks who got jobs in 1933 as a result of Baltimore's "Don't Buy Where You Can't Work" boycott.

"We boycotted all the A&P [grocery] stores in the northwest Baltimore ghetto," recalled Juanita Jackson Mitchell. Hundreds of young people marched in front of the stores, urging everyone not to shop there. The strategy worked. Within a few weeks, those A&P stores began hiring blacks. Changing other stores took longer. Some store owners got a local court to issue an order forbidding any picketing outside their stores, but people continued the boycott by simply not shopping at those stores. The boycott eventually led to more jobs for African Americans in neighborhood businesses, but black employment downtown remained limited. In 1938, the U.S. Supreme Court ruled that store owners couldn't do what those Baltimore storekeepers had done—block picketing at their stores. This ruling came in a case the NAACP argued on behalf of a similar Buy Where You Can Work campaign in Washington, D.C. The Supreme Court declared that it was all right for people to picket a store in order to protest against employment discrimination.

The Baltimore Young People's Forum did more than picket stores. It also invited guest speakers to come to their Friday night meetings. Anyone—young or old—could attend. "We brought all of the NAACP leaders and . . . historians, white and black from all over the country . . . to give us some ideas of how we might help ourselves change Baltimore," said Juanita Jackson Mitchell. "We became molders of thought . . . of a cohesive community single-mindedness on the part of the adults as well as the young people in the northwest community."

Her mother, Lillie May Carroll Jackson, was an advisor to the City-Wide Young People's Forum. She organized a parents group to help with the boycott and also provided guidance to the Forum. Mrs. Jackson was so successful at mobilizing community support for the young people that *Afro-American* editor Carl Murphy asked her to help reorganize Baltimore's NAACP chapter in 1935. That led to her being elected the chapter's president the same year. The activism of her daughters, combined with Mrs. Jackson's own energetic spirit, led to a dramatic turnaround for Baltimore's branch of the NAACP. Mrs. Jackson, who once remarked that "God opened my mouth and no man can shut it," served as the chapter's dynamic president for thirty-five years.

Under Mrs. Jackson's leadership, a volunteer job for which she received no pay, Baltimore's chapter became one of the NAACP's largest and most active. It grew from 100 members in 1935 to more than 17,000 about ten years later. Judge Robert Watts, who worked closely with Mrs. Jackson for many years, recalled that "she was a very persuasive person. . . . A lot of people didn't like her because she was so forceful—many whites just thought she was overbearing, but I think those that didn't like her respected her and that's all that she wanted."

An early victory under her watch came in 1936 when Maryland's highest court ruled that the University of Maryland Law School had to admit African Americans, although the rest of the university remained segregated and didn't integrate completely

TENNIS LESSON

Baltimore's Druid Hill Park used to have separate swimming pools and tennis courts for blacks and whites. To protest this, some young people organized an interracial tennis tournament at the park on July 11, 1948. A white teenager, Mitzi Freistat Swan, got a permit from the park office to hold the tournament on the whites-only tennis court. As soon as she and a black teen, Mary Coffee, walked onto the court, police arrested them and about twenty others. Their protest didn't end Jim Crow, but it highlighted the unfairness of segregation. Seven years later, the U.S. Supreme Court ended segregation at Baltimore's *public* parks, in a case argued by Juanita Jackson Mitchell. It would be nearly ten more years after that victory, however, before Jim Crow was booted out of the area's most popular *private* park, Gwynn Oak.

until the 1950s. A young Baltimore lawyer, Thurgood Marshall, argued the law school case for the NAACP. This was an impressive start for the local NAACP and for Thurgood Marshall, who went on a few years later to become the national director of all NAACP legal work. In 1967, he rose even higher, becoming the first African American justice on the U.S. Supreme Court.

Many black students who could now attend the University of Maryland Law School used their legal skills to score their own victories against Jim Crow. Among them was Mrs. Jackson's daughter Juanita. She earned her law degree in 1950, after working for several years organizing youth groups for the NAACP around the country. By then, she had married Clarence Mitchell, Jr., a former reporter for the *Afro-American* who had been the vice president of the City-Wide Young People's Forum when she was its president. In 1946, Mr. Mitchell began working as one of the NAACP's chief representatives in Washington. He continued lobbying for the NAACP in the nation's capital for nearly thirty years. Mrs.

Mitchell and another black Maryland Law School graduate, Robert Watts, served for many years as volunteer lawyers for Baltimore's NAACP, providing free legal help for civil rights protestors, including those at Gwynn Oak.

VOTING POWER

In the spring of 1942—the same year that a sound truck drove around town blaring out ads for Gwynn Oak Amusement Park—NAACP leader Lillie May Carroll Jackson and her daughter Juanita joined with about 150 local groups to organize a huge demonstration in Annapolis, the state capital. Some of their goals for this "March on Annapolis" were to protest police brutality against blacks in Baltimore and to call for the hiring of more African Americans as police officers, judges, and members of government boards. About 2,000 people traveled by car, bus, or train to Annapolis to present their complaints to the governor, who responded by appointing a commission to study problems in race relations. The March on Annapolis also led to more African American police officers being hired in Baltimore and to their being permitted to wear official police uniforms.

Mrs. Jackson was a member of this new state commission, but she soon resigned, irritated that it wasn't accomplishing much. She decided that she could be more effective as an outsider who would feel free to speak up and prod government officials into taking action. Her daughter Juanita noted that Mrs. Jackson "believed her role was as a gadfly to sting the system, to protest, to take the system into court to get the laws changed, to correct the wrongs in the system."

Mrs. Jackson realized that the black community needed to exert more political power. One way to do that was to have more African American voters. Baltimore's NAACP began a series of voter registration drives, directed by Juanita Jackson Mitchell. The number of Baltimore's black voters nearly doubled between 1940 and 1952. Nine thousand new voters signed up in 1943 alone.

All those new African American voters captured the attention of white politicians, including Theodore R. McKeldin, a forward-thinking lawyer who was elected mayor of Baltimore in 1943. After one term as mayor, he became the state's governor from 1951 to 1959, and then returned as mayor in 1963. He won these elections largely because of solid support from African American voters. His deep religious beliefs and his experiences as a youngster growing up poor made him sympathetic to the plight of African Americans. He supported equal rights and gave eloquent speeches about brotherhood, even preaching sermons in black churches. In 1944, during his first term as mayor, he did something unheard of in a Southern-leaning city: He appointed the first African American to serve on the city's school board. This was something the previous mayor had refused to do, despite being encouraged to make such an appointment by the NAACP and *Afro-American* editor Carl Murphy.

Mr. McKeldin continued appointing blacks to key posts throughout his years in office. As governor in 1957, he appointed E. Everett Lane to be the first black judge to serve on a state court in Maryland, while also appointing Robert Watts as a judge in Baltimore Traffic Court. In another bold move, Governor McKeldin issued an order in 1955 that ended segregation in the Maryland National Guard.

Some blacks criticized Theodore McKeldin for not doing more, but others praised him for doing what he could. "Mr. McKeldin was years ahead of his time. . . . one of the first politicians to recognize the inherent strength [of] the black community," said Rev. Marion C. Bascom, a key leader in Baltimore's civil rights struggles. Judge Watts added, "His eloquent way of preaching of the brotherhood of man became significant because he backed it up with action."

Of course, there was no way a single elected official could change a system as deeply entrenched as Jim Crow, especially because many whites seemed to like things the way they were. But having a mayor speak up for brotherhood set a different tone in Baltimore.

WHITE SUPPORTERS

Theodore McKeldin wasn't the only white Baltimorean who opposed Jim Crow. "There were people who were social liberals who took the position that you can't do the kinds of things that were done in the South because it wouldn't be right," explained Judge Robert Bell. "People who were very outspoken, who took reasonable positions and constituted a counterbalance to some of the others." Both the Urban League and the NAACP always had some white members. Juanita Jackson Mitchell noted, "There were always a few whites who braved the wrath and scorn and ostracism [of the white community] to work with my mother in the NAACP." Liberal whites also belonged to other organizations that weren't as activist as the NAACP but that often supported the efforts of activists and engaged in behind-the-scenes persuasion. Among such groups were Americans for Democratic Action, started in the 1940s, and Fellowship House, an interfaith educational organization that provided interracial classes in the arts.

In May 1944, some whites joined more than 700 African Americans at an African American church for a meeting of Baltimore's NAACP. An overflow crowd of about a thousand blacks stood outside the church, listening to the speeches on a loudspeaker. The main speaker was Eleanor Roosevelt. She and her husband, President Franklin Roosevelt, were popular with African Americans for speaking out against discrimination. President Roosevelt appointed blacks to important jobs in his administration and also ended job discrimination at factories that produced military equipment during World War II, a popular move with black Baltimoreans because many of the city's factories did military work. Mrs. Roosevelt said in her speech, "We must go forward together, we cannot be separate."

However, there was an added strain in Baltimore black-white relations which grew out of the fact that some department stores, with their clothes-buying restrictions, were owned by Jewish businessmen. Of course, these weren't the only Jim Crow department stores in town. Stores owned by non-Jewish whites had Jim Crow

Juanita Jackson Mitchell (in light-colored dress, looking at camera) with Eleanor Roosevelt outside a Baltimore church where Mrs. Roosevelt spoke at an NAACP meeting, May 1944.

rules, too. Even so, there developed a certain friction between the black and Jewish communities, even though both groups were victims of discrimination. The housing restrictions that prevented black families from moving into certain Baltimore neighborhoods kept Jewish families from living in some neighborhoods, too. In addition, for many years, local universities and private schools would admit only a small number of Jewish students, and many private clubs refused to have Jewish members. Perhaps because of these shared experiences, many in the Jewish community were strong civil rights supporters, including some who worked for those segregated department stores.

LEARNING TO SPEAK UP

Arthur Waskow, who graduated from an all-white Baltimore high school in 1950, found during his senior year that there were *two* citywide Future Teachers Associations: one for black students and one for whites. He wrote an editorial for the school newspaper condemning this example of segregation. The school administration wouldn't let it be published. His parents were civil rights supporters but told him that if he made a fuss about this, he might not get a college scholarship. "I agreed to keep my mouth shut. It's one of the things I'm ashamed of in my life. Sixty years later, I'm still ashamed," said Arthur Waskow, now a rabbi who speaks up often against injustice of all kinds.

Juanita Jackson Mitchell noted the contradictions: "Jewish people were always working with us on our protests. . . . Rabbis were always active with us. . . . There were Jewish lawyers who always came and worked with us on our cases." Yet she acknowledged, "We felt that the Jewish merchants as a class exploited us. . . . At the same time here were the liberal Jewish leaders, the Rabbis who were assisting us in our protests." Race relations in Baltimore were complex indeed.

Among the most outspoken white opponents of Jim Crow in Baltimore was Sidney Hollander, Sr., a Jewish business leader and the grandfather of Mike Furstenberg, who as a teenage protestor would be arrested at Gwynn Oak in 1963. Mr. Hollander owned a company that made drugstore items, from cough syrup to insect repellent. He was active in Baltimore's Urban League, served on the national board of the NAACP, and supported many charitable organizations that helped those who faced economic hardship and discrimination. In 1941, for his sixtieth birthday, his family set up the Sidney Hollander Foundation. Each year from 1946 to 1964, this foundation gave an award to the person or group that had made "an outstanding contribution toward the achievement of equal rights and opportunities" for African Americans in Maryland. "My grandfather felt strongly about ideas of social justice, equality, and interfaith communication," said Mike Furstenberg. "That was his life's work. My brothers, sisters, and cousins were brought up with this belief, and it followed naturally for me to be involved, too."

LOOKING FORWARD

Despite Baltimore's differences from cities farther south, when those handsome carousel horses first began circling round and round on Gwynn Oak's new merry-go-round in 1947, there was no way any African American youngster would be allowed to climb into one of the saddles.

Baltimore was starting to change, but much remained the same. On the plus side: The *Sun* earned the first Hollander Foundation Award in 1946 for editorials it wrote against Jim Crow and for agreeing not to list race anymore in its help-wanted ads. In addi-

A 1930s streetcar, with an ad for Gwynn Oak on the front.

tion, the NAACP had recently won a court case in 1945 that opened up librarian jobs for blacks in Baltimore's public libraries. On the down side: Jim Crow restrictions and job discrimination at other major employers were widespread. Local schools were still segregated, as were nearly all the city's restaurants, theaters, department stores, downtown businesses—and its most popular amusement park, Gwynn Oak.

However, in 1947, the same year that the new merry-go-round arrived at Gwynn Oak, seeds of change were being sown that would cause the eventual downfall of Jim Crow at the park sixteen years later. During the spring of 1947, cracks began appearing in the Jim Crow system. There was a major league breakthrough in the world of sports, as well as the national debut of a new organization that would lead the charge at Gwynn Oak.

"These discriminatory practices have no real basis in logic or common sense or fairness. . . . We must not accept the existing order if it is unjust."

—Theodore R. McKeldin, May 28, 1953, from the acceptance speech for his Hollander Foundation Award

© James Singewald

CHIPPING AWAY
AT JIM CROW
1947 to 1955

T HE YEAR 1947 MARKED both the beginning—and also the beginning of the end—of a whites-only career for Gwynn Oak's new merry-go-round. That spring, startling breakthroughs occurred which set in motion a course of events that would lead ultimately to the merry-go-round becoming a ride open to everyone.

One of that year's ground-breaking events occurred in Brooklyn, New York, on April 15. Jackie Robinson knocked a big hole in the Jim Crow system that day by joining the Brooklyn Dodgers, becoming the first African American on a major league baseball team. At first, some fans booed him, a few pitchers tried to bean him, diehard segregationists made death threats against him, and he had trouble finding hotel rooms when his team went on the road because so many hotels were off limits to African Americans. But by the end of the 1947 season, cheers drowned out boos as Jackie Robinson was honored as Rookie of the Year. Two years later, when a few additional African Americans were playing on other major league teams, he finished the

43

Jackie Robinson, April 1947, the month he became the first African American on a Major League Baseball team.

AP Photo/John Rooney

season as the National League's Most Valuable Player, with a league-leading batting average. Many sports fans were beginning to adjust to the idea that an end to the Jim Crow era might be coming, in the sports world at least, and maybe soon in other aspects of life as well.

What a difference from July 1944, when Jackie Robinson had been arrested in Texas for not moving to the back of a bus. At the time of his arrest, he was a second lieutenant in the Army, stationed in Texas, and was riding on a local bus to a nearby hospital. Buses that transported American soldiers during World War II were not supposed to discriminate against blacks, but many Southern bus drivers did so anyway, forcing black soldiers to take seats in the back. In 1944, bus drivers in North Carolina and Louisiana shot and killed black soldiers for not changing their seats. Lieutenant Robinson protested his arrest and the charges were dropped. He said, "I had learned that I was in two wars, one against the foreign enemy, the other against prejudice at home." That prejudice extended into the military itself, where African Americans could serve only in all-black units. For years, the NAACP had tried to have this policy changed. Finally, in 1948, President Harry Truman ordered an end to racial discrimination in the military, so that blacks and whites could serve side-by-side in the same units.

NEW GROUP—NEW IDEAS

Another event in the spring of 1947 that would have a big impact on Gwynn Oak's merry-go-round was the first major appearance on the national scene of a brand new civil rights group: the Congress of Racial Equality (CORE). Eventually, this new organization would lead the efforts to end segregation at Gwynn Oak, but first it had to develop and test out its special approach to challenging the Jim Crow system.

CORE got its start in 1942 in Chicago, founded by a small group of university students who believed in using peaceful means to solve problems. They were especially impressed with the ideas of Mohandas Gandhi, who for two decades had been leading a nonviolent protest movement in India. The year 1947 was an important one for Gandhi, too—the year his nonviolent protests achieved their goal of winning India its independence from Great Britain.

But before CORE made its 1947 debut on the national scene, it spent a few years trying out Gandhi's methods on a small scale, beginning in Chicago. In 1942, CORE's founders chose as one of their first targets a Chicago restaurant that refused to let black customers come in and eat. Committed to trying persuasion first, CORE members spoke with the restaurant's owner, asking him to admit African Americans. When that failed, they handed out fliers to customers entering the restaurant, asking them to speak up against discrimination at the restaurant.

When none of these tactics worked, about twenty CORE members—black and white—held a direct, nonviolent protest at the restaurant, doing what they felt Gandhi's followers would do: They had a sit-in. They walked in, sat down at tables, ordered food, and refused to leave until the restaurant served all of them.

The demonstrators had agreed to be nonviolent, not fight back or even talk back if provoked. That way they hoped they would be seen as the good guys, not a bunch of rowdy troublemakers. They thought a peaceful sit-in could change people's minds by showing the unfairness of denying people food because of skin color. As James Farmer, one of the African American founders of CORE, explained, "We . . . believed that truth alone, the transparent justice of our demands, would convert the segregationists, once they agreed to listen." This first CORE sit-in turned out to be a surprising success. Everyone got something to eat.

Encouraged by this success, CORE wanted to organize more protests like the sit-in—direct, nonviolent, public protests that put segregationists on the spot. They were unhappy with how little progress other groups had made in battling Jim Crow. They were especially impatient with the approach used by the NAACP. Although NAACP chapters sometimes sponsored picketing, its central strategy was quite different from CORE's. A primary focus of the NAACP was to remove the legal supports for Jim Crow. It tried to do this either by persuading public officials to do the right thing and end various aspects of segregation—or by having NAACP lawyers file challenges in courts, hoping to get judges to require an end to discrimination. However, court cases can drag on for years, one reason CORE didn't like a court-based approach.

But although CORE members complained about the slowness of court cases, they made use of a major NAACP Supreme Court victory to launch CORE's first big, national protest in the spring of 1947.

CORE'S 1947 ROLL-OUT

By early 1947, CORE had branches in about a dozen cities, although not yet in Baltimore. Some chapters had organized a few sit-ins and boycotts, but others hadn't done much. CORE's leaders felt it was time to try something on a bigger scale so more people could learn about their approach to ending Jim Crow. They decided to mount a protest that would highlight the differences between CORE and the NAACP by testing whether an NAACP Supreme Court victory in 1946 had actually made a difference.

That court case, *Morgan v. Virginia*, involved Irene Morgan, a Baltimore woman who had been arrested in Virginia in July 1944, the same month as Jackie Robinson, for much the same reason. This young African American woman had refused to give up her seat to a white person on a bus she was taking home to Maryland after visiting her mother in Virginia. NAACP lawyers appealed her arrest to the U.S. Supreme Court, which decided that Virginia had no right to arrest Ms. Morgan because she was on an interstate bus that traveled in other states besides Virginia. The court based its ruling on a section of the U.S. Constitution, the Commerce Clause, which says that only the national government can make rules for companies that do business with more than one state. Interstate buses are such a business. So states could not make laws about who sits where on interstate buses.

At first, many African Americans thought this court victory meant that the Jim Crow era would soon be over. However, Southern bus companies found a way to get around the Supreme Court. It had prohibited *laws* that a state might make but had said nothing about *rules* that a bus company might make. Southern bus companies simply made their own Jim Crow rules and continued to force blacks to sit in the back of a bus.

CORE felt that the bus companies' "end-run" around the Supreme Court proved that court victories alone would not end Jim Crow. Also needed was a way to change the public's attitudes so that companies would not dare to defy the spirit of a Supreme Court ruling. So in April 1947 (the same month as Jackie Robinson's first major league at-bat), sixteen CORE volunteers set out on a two-week bus trip through four Southern states to see if the *Morgan v. Virginia* court victory had really changed bus travel.

These CORE bus riders—eight white men and eight black men—split into two interracial groups to take Trailways and Greyhound buses through Virginia, North Carolina, Kentucky, and Tennessee. They chose only states in the northern part of the South, feeling that traveling farther South would be too dangerous. On this trip, which they named the Journey of Reconciliation, black volunteers would sit toward the front of a bus. When a driver asked them to move to the rear, they would explain that because of the recent Supreme Court decision, blacks had the right to sit up front. Before heading off on this adventure, the volunteers took part in a two-day workshop to learn nonviolent protest

Nine of CORE's Journey of Reconciliation volunteers in Richmond, Virginia, at the start of their bus journey, April 1947. In later years, Jim Peck (fourth from left) took part in demonstrations at Gwynn Oak. Bayard Rustin (fourth from right) became the chief organizer of the 1963 March on Washington.

techniques—how to remain nonviolent and protect themselves should they be attacked.

The volunteers knew they risked being arrested, as Homer Plessy knew he would be when he challenged Jim Crow more than fifty years earlier in Louisiana. By the end of CORE's two-week journey, there had been a dozen arrests. Most of the volunteers paid a fine and got out of jail, but four were sentenced to a month's hard labor and had to work on prison road-repair crews.

By the end of this bus campaign, CORE had proved that the NAACP's 1946 Supreme Court victory had not changed interstate bus travel. Buses were still segregated. Most of the drivers and regular passengers on the buses that CORE volunteers took didn't even seem to know about the Supreme Court's *Morgan* decision.

However, CORE didn't end Jim Crow, either. The arrests earned some publicity, but not enough to fire up the public to demand change. It would be several years before CORE learned how to do that.

Yet, CORE was now better known. New branches opened, including the one in Baltimore that would eventually inspire enough people to demand an end to Jim Crow at Gwynn Oak Amusement Park.

CORE COMES TO BALTIMORE

CORE's Baltimore chapter began in 1953, six years after the Journey of Reconciliation bus protest. Herbert Kelman, a white psychologist, started the Baltimore chapter by bringing together an interracial group of about twenty-five fellow Baltimoreans who shared his interest in Gandhi's philosophy of nonviolent protest. Several of the group's black founding members were also active in the NAACP, including lawyer Robert Watts, who had started Morgan State College's NAACP chapter when he was an undergraduate there. The head of Morgan's NAACP chapter in 1953 was also among Baltimore CORE's founders, as was piano teacher Adah Jenkins, who later became a columnist for the *Afro-American* newspaper. White founding members included local high school teacher Ben Everingham.

The Baltimore CORE chapter had an amazing string of early successes. Its members focused first on low-cost variety stores whose lunch counters refused to serve black customers. Like fast food restaurants today, these lunch counters were places to have quick, inexpensive meals. The Baltimore activists followed the same plan that CORE had used in Chicago. First, they would test out the stores, to learn which ones discriminated against blacks. Many of the stores allowed African Americans to buy things, just not sit down at the lunch counter to eat.

After CORE identified which stores refused to serve food to African Americans, the next step was persuasion. That was all that was needed at the first variety store they targeted in January 1953, a Kresge's store. CORE sent a letter to the manager of a Baltimore Kresge's, protesting the store's segregation policy. The store manager sent the letter to his national headquarters, which told him to stop discriminating against blacks. Then Kresge's national office contacted CORE and suggested that its volunteers visit the store again. They did and were glad to find that the store had dropped Jim Crow. No sit-in was required.

To follow up on this victory, CORE told the manager of a downtown Woolworth's store about the change at Kresge's. As a result, the Woolworth's opened up its lunch counter—another easy win. During the rest of 1953 and on into 1954, Baltimore CORE integrated lunch counters at two other variety store chains—McCrory's and Grant's—although CORE had to use sit-ins to change these stores.

CORE was on a roll. It teamed up in 1953 with Morgan State College students, who wanted to end segregation at the Northwood Shopping Center, which was a short walk from the Morgan campus on the northeast edge of Baltimore. Letter-writing did the trick at the shopping center's Kresge's store, but wasn't enough to change the center's Read's drug store. There were several other Read's drug stores throughout the Baltimore area. Morgan students spent about eight months staging sit-ins off and on at the lunch counter of the Read's near the Morgan campus. At the same time, Morgan officials and members of CORE began negotiating with store managers to try to solve the problem.

In January 1955, about six to eight Morgan students were downtown waiting to take a bus. They decided to hold a spur-of-the-moment sit-in at the lunch counter of the Read's drug store that was at the intersection where they were standing, the corner of Howard and Lexington Streets. The weather was cold and the students were hungry. "We just thought, 'We're going to go in and sit down and see what happens,'" said Dr. Helena Hicks, then a first-year Morgan student. No sooner did they sit down at the lunch

MEETING MARIAN ANDERSON

African Americans couldn't perform at Baltimore's Lyric Theater until January 1954, when Marian Anderson held a recital there. At first, the Lyric said no to her recital. A concert hall in Washington, D.C., had done the same thing in 1939. Back then, President and Mrs. Franklin Roosevelt worked with the NAACP to move Ms. Anderson's concert to the Lincoln Memorial. This time, Baltimore's Commission on Human Relations persuaded the Lyric to let her perform. But what about an after-concert reception? Hotels and restaurants were still segregated. Sidney Hollander, Sr., held the reception at his home. "Meeting Marian Anderson and having her come to the house was the high point of my early youth," said his grandson Mike Furstenberg, age eight in 1954 and a teen in 1963 when he was arrested during a Gwynn Oak protest.

counter than the store manager asked them to leave. The students stayed a few minutes and then left, but they had made their point, as had the students holding sit-ins at the Read's near their campus. Members of CORE and Morgan officials followed up by speaking with the owner of the Read's drug stores and managed to persuade him to drop Jim Crow. A few days after that downtown sit-in, Read's opened its lunch counters to everyone—black and white—at all its stores in the Baltimore area.

This success showed the power of combining an attention-getter—the sit-ins—with solid, behind-the-scenes negotiations. A two-pronged approach like this would pay off years later at Gwynn Oak, too.

A NEW FORCE IN TOWN

These sit-ins didn't receive much press coverage outside of Baltimore, although they earned CORE a Hollander Award in 1953.

Nor did they spark a wave of copycat sit-ins around the country, as happened five years later, in 1960, when North Carolina college students did very much the same thing that Morgan students had done. (See chapter 5.) By 1960, reporters had grown more interested in covering civil rights, and the stories they wrote helped spread the word about the North Carolina sit-ins.

Even though Baltimore's 1950s sit-ins didn't get nationwide attention, they were important to the growth of the civil rights movement in the city. They led directly to the birth of a major, local protest group. Originally Morgan students' protest activities had been an offshoot of the college's student government social action committee. But in 1955, the Morgan administration felt it would be best if this type of student activism wasn't an official school activity. Douglas Sands, one of the student protest leaders, met with Morgan's president. It was decided that the students would form an independent organization, separate from the college. They called their new group the Civic Interest Group (CIG). Most CIG members attended Morgan, but sometimes white students from other Baltimore colleges participated, too, as did some high school students.

CIG played a key role over the next decade in pushing local activists to be more daring in their choice of tactics. Although based in Baltimore, CIG established contacts with student organizations in other states, encouraging them to join some CIG protests. When members of CIG graduated from college, they often went on to volunteer with other Baltimore protest groups, including CORE and the NAACP.

WORKING TOGETHER

By the mid-1950s, the major organizations were in place that would lead Baltimore's struggle against Jim Crow for the next decade, including the soon-to-be launched campaign aimed at Gwynn Oak Amusement Park. The key players were the NAACP, CORE, CIG, and the Interdenominational Ministerial Alliance, a group of activist ministers. Other groups that helped in supporting roles included the Urban League and Fellowship House, an interracial educational organization.

The NAACP was more organized than CORE or CIG and had access to more funds. Although Baltimore's NAACP president, Lillie May Carroll Jackson, received no salary and the chapter depended in large part on volunteer lawyers to provide free legal services, the chapter raised money from its members. It often used those funds to help protestors from other groups when they were arrested at demonstrations. Ministers and their congregations also provided financial support for protestors, in addition to making church buildings available for meetings.

Sometimes conflicts over tactics arose among these groups. In addition, CIG students were fiercely independent and did not want to be supervised by adults from any of the other groups. Despite their differences, there was a remarkable degree of cooperation among the groups over the next decade. "There was rivalry, as you'd get with any groups competing for the same goal," said Charles Mason, who took part in CIG activities as a student at Morgan before volunteering with CORE in the early 1960s. "Egos were always around, with people saying, 'You should do it my way.' But when it came down to the wire, they all worked together in presenting a united front. Some churches approved of what we did, but some thought we were rocking the boat, saying, 'Now is not the time,' or saying for us to wait until this or that happens. We thought now *was* the time. If not now, when?"

"The youngsters kind of felt that we were too slow, the NAACP method . . . [going] to the mayors and the governors and . . . to court. They said the courts were slow," recalled Judge Robert Watts. He noted that Lillie May Carroll Jackson felt "hurt" by the students' attitudes and didn't always like their tactics, but he added, "She played a very significant role in their movement. . . . She supplied the lawyers. She gave the contributions." She often provided bail money so protestors could be released promptly after being arrested. Judge Watts noted that CIG and CORE "didn't have any money and every time they got locked up, who did they call . . . the NAACP."

Bayard Rustin picketing in Baltimore at Ford's Theatre, 1948. In front of him is Patricia Jackson, wife of Juanita Jackson Mitchell's brother.

Sometimes Baltimore's NAACP ventured into CORE-like direct action, too, as when it organized picketing at Ford's Theatre, the main local theater that brought Broadway shows to town. African Americans could sit only in the last rows of the top balcony. They weren't even allowed to walk through the theater's main lobby to reach their seats but had to use a side entrance. From the late 1940s until 1952, whenever there were shows at Ford's, the NAACP had picketers in front of the theater holding signs that asked people to boycott Ford's.

Among the Ford's Theatre picketers were the NAACP's Lillie May Carroll Jackson, Juanita Jackson Mitchell, her husband, Clarence, piano teacher Adah Jenkins, several Morgan students, and a few college professors. Some high school students participated, too, including Robert Kaufman, a 16-year-old tenth grader who heard about the picketing in 1947 when he joined an interracial, interfaith youth group at Fellowship House, which Adah Jenkins had helped found. He began picketing at Ford's Saturday matinee performances. He and Ms. Jenkins helped extend the reach of the boycott by writing letters to famous actors and playwrights, asking them not to take part in shows at Ford's. Theodore McKeldin, then Maryland's governor, worked with the state's newly reorganized Commission on Interracial Problems and Relations to negotiate a settlement that led to Ford's dropping Jim Crow in 1952. Governor McKeldin earned a Hollander Foundation Award for this victory and for other actions he had taken to advance the cause of "equal rights and opportunities," such as appointing African Americans to various state government positions.

PRESSURED TO DO RIGHT

The NAACP as a whole achieved an even bigger victory two years later, in 1954, doing what it did best: attack Jim Crow in the U.S. Supreme Court. This 1954 triumph energized civil rights supporters around the country and helped set the stage for other protests against Jim Crow, such as those that would soon be starting at Gwynn Oak Amusement Park.

Led by Thurgood Marshall, then the national organization's chief lawyer, the NAACP legal team managed to persuade the Supreme Court in 1954 to outlaw segregation in public schools throughout the country. This case, *Brown v. Board of Education*, was named for Oliver Brown, a Kansas father who didn't want his daughter going to a segregated school. On May 17, 1954, the Supreme Court declared that separate, segregated public schools for blacks were illegal.

This court ruling attacked the main legal support for Jim Crow—the separate-but-equal policy that dated back to the *Plessy* case of 1896. (See chapter 2). The Supreme Court explained that separate schools could never be equal because "the policy of separating the races is usually interpreted as denoting the inferiority of" African Americans, which can affect "the motivation of a child to learn." The justices ruled that such segregated schools deprived African American students "of the equal protection of the laws guaranteed by the Fourteenth Amendment" to the U.S. Constitution.

The court also commented on the psychological harm that segregation could cause, noting that to separate young people "solely because of their race generates a feeling of inferiority as to their status in the community that may affect their hearts and minds." Such a concern would seem to require an end to Jim Crow in every phase of American life. Sadly, that would require many more years. Nevertheless, this court decision marked an important step forward.

Actually, fifteen Baltimore students had already integrated one of the city's high schools two years before the Supreme Court's *Brown* decision. The Urban League had led the effort to achieve this 1952 Baltimore breakthrough, with help from the NAACP and other local groups, including Americans for Democratic Action. They persuaded the Baltimore school board to let a few black students into an advanced program at "Poly," the city's prestigious all-boys math-and-science Polytechnic High School. The school board made this change after concluding that it was impossible to set up a truly equal advanced program at a separate school. The NAACP then tried to have African American girls admitted to an advanced program at the all-girls Western High School and to have blacks admitted to a specialized vocational high school. The school board turned down these two requests. The NAACP followed up with court challenges, but the Supreme Court announced its 1954 school decision before those challenges were resolved.

The Poly case had given the nine members of the school board a head start in thinking about the unfairness of segregation. Serving on the board was a volunteer activity, and members had other jobs. Dr. Bernard Harris, the school board's only black member,

Courtesy Afro-American Newspapers Archives

Everett Sherman, Jr. (right), at Baltimore's Polytechnic High School, which he helped integrate in September 1952, two years before the Supreme Court's 1954 Brown v. Board of Education *ruling.*

was a surgeon. Walter Sondheim, Jr., the board's president, was a department store executive. "None of us, in our hearts, really believed that the best education could be obtained in the long run in a segregated school system," said Mr. Sondheim.

The school board members all believed in equal rights. But before the Supreme Court's decision, they felt they couldn't end school segregation because they had to obey the city law that said blacks and whites had to attend separate schools. However, once the Supreme Court acted, they felt free to follow their hearts. They discussed the situation privately and checked with the city's lawyer to make sure the Supreme Court decision overruled the city's Jim Crow school law. Then in early June, less than three weeks after the Court had announced its decision, the school board met and voted unanimously to end segregation in Baltimore schools when the new school year started that September. Catholic schools followed their lead. So did some private schools, including the Park School, which Mary Sue Welcome entered that fall as its first African American student.

"It's interesting that there was practically no hesitation on the part of the School Board in deciding to desegregate the schools and to do it immediately," said Mr. Sondheim. Changing a long-entrenched system is hard, especially when there's likely to be fierce opposition, as board members feared there might be in some Baltimore neighborhoods. With major changes such as this one, it helps to have some kind of outside pressure that can support taking such a big step forward. In this case, the pressure came from the Supreme Court and from the threat of more lawsuits by the local NAACP. This pressure not only prodded board members to take action but also gave them a way to answer complaints: A Supreme Court order must be obeyed. "Our school board was somewhat relieved by the Supreme Court decision," said Mr. Sondheim. It strengthened their commitment to do the right thing. Finding just the right kind of outside pressure to exert would be the secret to achieving victory at Gwynn Oak, too.

BALTIMORE TAKES THE LEAD

Baltimore was one of the first cities in the Southern part of the nation to officially end school segregation. It rolled out its new policy citywide in September 1954. Baltimore was way ahead of other cities in Maryland, too. The NAACP's Lillie May Carroll Jackson traveled around with state with lawyer Robert Watts, speaking to school officials, urging them to follow the city's lead.

Washington, D.C., also ended school segregation that fall. St. Louis schools dropped segregation gradually during that year and the next. However, many Southern cities refused to end segregated education for several years. In Little Rock, Arkansas, it took federal troops to integrate the schools. President Dwight Eisenhower sent soldiers of the Army's 101st Airborne Division to Little Rock in September 1957 to protect nine black students as they integrated one of the city's high schools. In Virginia, legislators passed laws to oppose the Supreme Court's order—Massive Resistance laws, which threatened to close any public school that integrated. Only after a court ruled those laws unconstitutional did a few Virginia schools begin integrating in 1959. But by 1963, nearly ten years after the Supreme Court decision, more than a thousand school districts in several Southern states still hadn't ended segregation.

Baltimore already had a policy of letting parents and students decide which schools to attend, and this plan was followed in 1954 as well. Nobody was forced to attend an integrated school. Fewer than three percent of the city's black students decided to enroll in formerly all-white schools that fall, and only six white youngsters went to formerly all-black schools. Even so, nearly one-third of the city's schools wound up with some degree of integration that year, with black and white students attending classes together.

This experiment in citywide, integrated education in Baltimore went fairly well at first, but toward the end of September, trouble broke out. Some white parents and students marched in front of several schools, carrying signs against integration. In a few cases, white segregationist protestors harassed and even attacked black students. Things were especially tense at Southern High School, in a white, working-class part of town. This school had more than 1,700 white students that fall and only thirty-nine blacks, but those were enough to spark opposition from some in the neighborhood.

The white opponents to integration were inspired in part by heavy coverage in Baltimore newspapers of protests against the desegregation of schools in the town of Milford in the neighboring state of Delaware. Segregationists there urged whites to boycott the schools. Threats were phoned in to Milford school board members. The town dropped integration for that school year. The leader of the Delaware segregationists was in contact with Baltimoreans and came to Maryland to speak at a rally.

These kinds of segregationist protests affected Juanita Jackson Mitchell's son Keiffer, an eighth grader, who was the only

© Bettmann/Corbis

Integration of Baltimore's public schools went well at first, as seen in this photo taken at P.S. 99 in early September 1954.

Courtesy Baltimore Sun

In late September 1954, scattered protests against integration broke out in Baltimore, such as this one by people who didn't want Southern High School to be integrated.

black student that year at Gwynns Falls Park Junior High. Clarence Mitchell, Jr., the boy's father, escorted his son to school for about the first six weeks. Even so, white kids roughed up Keiffer on the playground one day during recess. The situation grew more dangerous toward the end of the last week in September when a white man punched Keiffer in the face as he walked into school. The following Monday morning, when Mr. Mitchell saw a crowd of segregationists marching in front of the school, he went home and called the police. Then he made a sign that said on one side "I AM AN AMERICAN TOO." He wrote on the sign's other side: "THIS IS MY COUNTRY TOO." Mr. Mitchell returned to his son's school and walked in front of the building with that sign, staging his own one-man demonstration. Police persuaded some of the segregationist picketers to leave.

That evening, Baltimore's police commissioner announced on TV that the police would arrest anyone who demonstrated near any public school. Lawyers had uncovered an old Maryland law that said it was illegal to interfere with the operation of the schools. The threat of being arrested put an end to the segregationist protests.

"I got abusive telephone calls, of course. I got some abusive mail," said school board president, Walter Sondheim, Jr. "We prepared a statement . . . saying schools were open and were going to stay open." He added that "one of the best things about the whole situation was the calm and restraint shown by the black community. . . . because the name calling that went on and the things that were said were enough to provoke anybody. . . . In retrospect, our troubles lasted only a few days. The kids were magnificent! . . . The captain of the football team and the president of the class walked out of Southern High School . . . acting as kind of a bodyguard escort" for black students.

As Keiffer Mitchell discovered, attending a previously all-white school wasn't easy. "I was the only black in all my classes," said Marie Williams, who went to Baltimore's all-girls Eastern High School and would later play a role in helping to organize the 1963 protests at Gwynn Oak. "I had one good white friend. The rest of them could care less. I didn't bother. I was there for education. I had to prove that I had the ability to keep up with them. Those were hard years, but it was worth it. You came out knowing that you are a trouper."

A love of art helped Keiffer Mitchell survive eighth grade in 1954 as the first—and only—black student that year at Gwynns Falls Park Junior High School. The school's art room and art teacher introduced this budding young artist to many more art materials than had been available at the segregated school he used to attend. He proved to his new junior high that talent is colorblind when a picture of a holiday scene that he had created was chosen for the cover of the school newspaper in December 1954. During high school, he found another interest—science—and eventually became a doctor, but he still draws and paints in his spare time.

"There was a good out-pouring of pride on the part of Baltimoreans that Baltimore was [one of] the first . . . to respond in this affirmative way to the Supreme Court decision," recalled Mr. Sondheim. The Hollander Award that year went to two school officials who had worked hard to keep the peace: Dr. John H. Fischer, superintendent of Baltimore schools, and John Schwatka, principal of Southern High School.

ON TO GWYNN OAK

By the end of 1955, Baltimore's Jim Crow system had a few dents in it. The city had survived its first year with desegregated schools. College students had managed to end discrimination at all of the city's Read's drug stores. Lunch counters at many low-cost variety stores had also been integrated. However, big, expensive, downtown department stores still had Jim Crow rules. So did most of the city's restaurants, movie theaters, and hotels.

Jim Crow also remained the order of the day at Gwynn Oak Amusement Park, despite a comment its owner made about the Supreme Court's *Brown v. Board of Education* school decision. When the court's ruling was announced in May 1954, the *Afro-*

American asked local officials for their reactions. Baltimore's mayor, Thomas D'Alesandro, Jr., was in the hospital. Filling in as temporary mayor was none other than Arthur B. Price, Sr., the owner of Gwynn Oak Amusement Park. He had been elected to the Baltimore City Council in the 1940s, became City Council president in 1951, and filled in as acting mayor when necessary. Mr. Price told the *Afro* reporter, "As good citizens, the Baltimore city administration will certainly follow the edict of the Supreme Court. As good citizens what else could we do?"

Apparently Mr. Price's commitment to being a "good citizen" didn't extend to applying the spirit of that Supreme Court ruling to his own amusement park.

Members of Baltimore CORE were ready to try to persuade him to change his mind. If kids could go to school together, why not do other things together, such as ride round and round on a merry-go-round?

CORE's Gwynn Oak campaign was about to begin.

1955 SCORECARD

In 1955 Baltimore was a city of a million people, one quarter of whom were black.

Newly integrated, 1946 to 1955. Many schools; some lunch counters; public housing; Ford's and Lyric theaters; two movie theaters; fire and police departments; bus drivers; city-owned golf courses, tennis courts, beaches, and pools; Baltimore Medical Society; Maryland National Guard; Maryland Teachers Association; Maryland Legislature (three blacks elected in 1954); Baltimore City Council (one black elected in 1955).

Still segregated. Many Baltimore hospitals; nearly all (91 percent) of "establishments that sell goods or services to the public" (restaurants, hotels, movie theaters, stores); many businesses; most private parks.

"We have never understood how the All Nations Day [festival] was so named when it welcomes no black peoples."

—Editorial, *Baltimore Afro-American*, September 1, 1962

© James Singewald

FIRST STEPS
AT GWYNN OAK

1955 to 1961

N EWLY ENERGIZED BY THE 1954 Supreme Court school desegregation ruling, Baltimore CORE members turned their
attention to Gwynn Oak Amusement Park.

Their first step, as in earlier projects, was to try persuasion.
They spoke with Gwynn Oak officials to see if the park might be
ready to drop Jim Crow. Persuasion didn't work.

Next, CORE sent groups of blacks and whites into the park to
buy tickets. They were turned away. Then during the summer of
1955, a few CORE members began picketing, walking back and
forth in front of the park, carrying signs and handing out leaflets
to park customers, urging them to tell the park's owners to end
segregation. These efforts failed, too.

So CORE moved on to the next stage—an official demonstration, based on Gandhi's ideas of nonviolent protest. CORE chose a
day when plenty of people would be at the park to hear their message, the day of the park's annual All Nations Day Festival. Gwynn
Oak had been holding this festival on Labor Day weekend for
the past four years, and it had become one of the park's biggest

money-makers. The year before, in 1954, about 40,000 people had crowded into the park for the festival.

Crowds weren't the only reason CORE chose this day. The festival provided a stark example of Jim Crow's unfairness—and its absurdity. The festival supposedly celebrated countries from around the world, a "carnival of cultures" it was called. Each year, the park's owners invited embassies of foreign countries to send representatives to the festival. These special guests, dressed in their nation's traditional costumes, performed their country's favorite dances and songs. They also brought along examples of the country's handicrafts and foods. Local Baltimoreans whose families came from other nations also brought examples of their homeland's culture.

However, Gwynn Oak's managers didn't seem to know the meaning of the word "all." They invited representatives to come to the festival from countries in Asia, Europe, Central and South America, the Middle East, the South Pacific—from "all" parts of the world except one.

They didn't invite black Africans to come and share their culture.

They didn't invite any Baltimoreans of African ancestry, either.

How could there be an All Nations Day Festival that didn't include "all" nations?

CORE members were sure that if they just pointed out the contradiction between the festival's name and the restrictive admission policy of the park, people would see the unfairness. That might help change people's attitudes, not only about excluding blacks from the park, but about the injustice of Jim Crow in other aspects of Baltimore life as well.

THE PROTESTS BEGIN

On Sunday, September 4, 1955, the first day of that year's All Nations Day Festival, about forty CORE members showed up at Gwynn Oak Amusement Park—blacks and whites, mostly adults, with some children there, too. For an hour they picketed, walk-

A sign at Gwynn Oak Amusement Park.

Courtesy Afro-American Newspapers Archives

ing peacefully back and forth in front of the entrance to the park. They carried signs with messages on them that called attention to the park's Jim Crow rules: "WE'RE AMERICANS ALL," "WHY ARE NEGROES NOT PERMITTED TO ATTEND ALL NATIONS DAY?" and "WHY ARE NEGROES NOT ADMITTED TO GWYNN OAK PARK?"

The park's managers refused to change. The picketing earned only a short, three-paragraph story in the *Sun*. An article in the *Afro-American* newspaper quoted Arthur B. Price, Jr., a son of the park's owner, as saying that he wasn't going to change the park's rules until other Baltimore businesses did, too. "We have to do just what other people are doing," he said. "Let the restaurants and hotels take the lead. We aren't going to be pioneers."

By then the three Price sons—David, James and Arthur, Jr.— managed the park. Their father had become too busy with politics as president of the Baltimore City Council. A few months before CORE's first All Nations Day demonstration, he had been campaigning to be elected mayor of Baltimore. He ran in the Democratic primary against his longtime political rival, the current mayor, Thomas D'Alesandro, Jr. Mr. Price lost by a huge margin. During the campaign, he had positioned himself as a reform-minded candidate. He even had the support of some in the African American community because he had voted for an Equal Opportunities Bill and promised, if elected mayor, to appoint blacks to city commissions. Those pro-black political stands make it all the more puzzling that his amusement park continued its Jim Crow rules. But cling to Jim Crow it did, even after he died in 1957 and his three sons became the park's owners.

MORE OF THE SAME

For the next six years, from 1956 to 1961, CORE kept trying to use persuasion with the Price brothers. Each year, when persuasion failed, CORE set up a picket line in front of the park during the All Nations Day Festival. In 1956, the second year of picketing, protestors handed out leaflets that posed this question: "If the American Negro can fight and die in battle for our country, why can't

Courtesy Afro-American Newspapers Archives

he be admitted to All Nation's Day?" Sometimes officials from CORE's national office came down from New York to help, but most picketers were Baltimoreans. Usually there were not more than a few dozen demonstra-

At the 1958 All Nations Day Festival, CORE picketers tried to buy tickets at Gwynn Oak, but were turned away by police.

tors each time. The results were always the same. The park's owners refused to drop Jim Crow.

No black youngsters would catch a ride on Gwynn Oak's merry-go-round until CORE found a way to force the Price brothers to change.

During the third year of picketing—1957—piano teacher Adah Jenkins, then CORE's vice-chairwoman, tried to bargain with the Price brothers. She suggested having a black musician perform at the festival as a "first step." The owners refused. She also tried to round up more picketers by sending letters to a hundred individuals and groups. Only about thirty protestors showed up. Some were members of CORE. A few came from the NAACP and other groups, including the American Legion and the Women's International League for Peace and Freedom. "This is an educational demonstration," Ms. Jenkins explained. "We are working in the spirit of good will and nonviolence. We are always ready to negotiate."

However, the park's owners had no interest in negotiating. They felt no pressure to change. CORE's picketers showed up usually only one weekend a year and stayed for such a short time that they didn't hurt business at the park. In fact, Gwynn Oak was doing so well that the Price brothers were investing money to add more rides and build new pavilions. They also created a bigger parking lot. By the mid-1950s, World War II gas rationing was a thing of the past. Automobile use rose steadily and more people came to Gwynn Oak by car. Streetcar ridership declined so much that the transit company began eliminating streetcar lines, replacing them with buses. The trolley line that went past Gwynn Oak shut down for good in August 1955, shortly before CORE's first All Nations Day protest. Much was changing at Gwynn Oak—but not its Jim Crow rules.

In 1958, the All Nations Day picketing at Gwynn Oak took a new turn. In addition to an interracial group of more than a dozen demonstrators picketing outside the park, two African American CORE members tried to enter the park with some white companions. A police officer and the park's private guards quickly led the

A streetcar on one of its last runs past Gwynn Oak's roller coaster, August 1955, shortly before that streetcar line was discontinued.

protestors out of the park. The guards also forced reporters and news photographers to leave the park and stop taking photos. The protestors weren't arrested, but they had to listen to insulting comments directed at them by some white customers and the park's private guards. The news story in the *Sun* was longer than in earlier years, but the reporter noted that few of the thousands of customers at the festival were aware of the demonstration or had noticed the protestors being removed from the park. The demonstration hadn't made much of an impact. The article went on to describe the festival itself—the wide variety of exotic foreign foods and handicrafts, along with colorfully costumed representatives from nineteen different nations, none from Africa, of course.

FIVE ARRESTS

Even the next year, in 1959, when five of CORE's forty protestors were arrested and another was beaten, the All Nations Day strategy failed to spark a public outcry against Jim Crow. Five demonstrators had managed to walk past the park's private security guards at that year's festival and stroll inside the park for about twenty minutes. When they tried to buy tickets at the ticket booth, a guard stopped them. Some of the park's white customers noticed what was going on and began shouting insults at the five protestors who had dared to enter the park: two women (an 18-year-old African American and an older white woman) and three men in their 20s (one black and two white). Soon about 500 people had joined the hostile crowd surrounding these five CORE volunteers.

When Baltimore County police officers arrived, they led the older woman and the teenager out of the park to be arrested. The three men dropped to the ground and refused to move. Police carried out one man. Arresting the other two men was harder because they had locked arms. As police dragged those two from the park, some in the hostile mob hit and kicked the two men and then beat up a sixth protestor as well. CORE had held workshops to train its volunteers to remain nonviolent and not fight back. The training worked. They stayed nonviolent.

The arrests were reported in fairly long news stories, in the *Sun* and in a few out-of-town newspapers, too. The *New York Times* reported that some in the mob taunted the demonstrators by calling up images of the South's historic way of dealing with agitators—lynching—by shouting, "Get them! Get a rope!"

A Baltimore County judge later found the five CORE members guilty of disturbing the peace and fined them twenty-five dollars each, despite the best efforts of Robert Watts, the NAACP lawyer who handled their case. He appealed the convictions. Finally, in 1965 the U.S. Supreme Court considered the case but refused to overturn the convictions.

The hecklers who attacked the picketers were never arrested or punished. One Baltimorean who was upset by such unfairness wrote a letter that was published in the *Sun* in September 1959: "I am amazed to see no indignation over the fact that those people who were peacefully exercising the time-honored American method of protest by picketing were arrested, while their assailants . . . went unpunished." That was about it for public outrage.

CORE's 1959 All Nations Day protest at Gwynn Oak

RIGHT: *These five protestors who entered the park were all arrested (from left): Joseph C. Sheehan, James L. Lacy, Dale H. Drews, Juretha Z. Joyner, and Mrs. Giles E. Brown.*

BELOW: *The women were led out by an officer (note the handcuffs). The men refused to walk and had to be carried.*

Photos on this page courtesy Baltimore Sun

A NEW STRATEGY

CORE's strategy wasn't working. They needed a better approach. It would be a few years before they found one.

At the next two All Nations Day Festivals—in 1960 and 1961— CORE went back to its original plan, having a small group picket outside the park, being careful not to be arrested. A few picketers also showed up on the park's opening day in the spring of 1960. The picketers at these protests carried signs, such as the eloquent one held by Verda Welcome at the 1960 All Nations Day protest. She had recently become the first black woman elected to the Maryland House of Delegates. Her sign read: "ALL MEN ARE CRE-ATED EQUAL. DOES ANYONE PRACTICE WHAT 1 PREACH? THE WORLD IS LISTENING." Those signs, no matter how powerful their message, did not change the park.

In September 1960, in a story about that year's All Nations Day picketing, the *Sun* reported that Arthur Price, Jr., said that opening the park to blacks would be "economic suicide." He feared that integration would make his white customers stop coming to the park.

In that same 1960 *Sun* article, a CORE official explained the goal of the Gwynn Oak picketing: "We are not looking for arrests or sensational publicity. We are simply protesting the park's policy and we want to convince the public that it is wrong."

These two comments in that news story—one by the owner and the other by the CORE official—provided clues for how CORE could succeed at Gwynn Oak in the future.

First, the comments by the CORE official described fairly well the strategy that had been used for six All Nations Day protests. Perhaps avoiding "sensational publicity" wasn't such a good idea if the goal was to change public opinion. A demonstration would have a greater chance of making an impact if a lot of people found out about it through news reports. In order to attract reporters, it would help if the demonstration involved something especially unusual or dramatically newsworthy.

In addition, the CORE official might have wanted to rethink the idea that they were "not looking for arrests." Baltimore CORE

MAKING A POINT

"My mother, who was active in the League of Women Voters, would take my sister and me on civil rights demonstrations throughout our childhood," said Margaret Levi, who remembers being at one at Gwynn Oak. When she was young, her mother "made us dress up and wear matching outfits the way kids did in those days [1950s], to my sister's and my infinite and continued embarrassment. But we looked very well put-together, very middle class. Part of what my mother and her friends were trying to convey was that this was a movement that was supported by the white middle class as well as by those who were immediately affected by the inequities of racial segregation." Her family also made a point of not going to Jim Crow restaurants, theaters, and businesses.

members were committed to Gandhi's protest philosophy and had mastered the nonviolent part. Going to jail for challenging unfair laws was another important part of Gandhi's strategy. The more arrests the better, because "filling the jails," as Gandhi's method is often described, would cause stress and embarrassment to those in power, and perhaps make them willing to negotiate a solution.

The other helpful clue in that 1960 *Sun* article was the Gwynn Oak owner's fear of "economic suicide." So far, CORE's protests had not cramped Gwynn Oak's style, nor lessened its profits. Maybe CORE could find a way to show the owner that "economic suicide" would come from sticking with segregation, not from dropping it.

"MAKING IT UP AS THEY WENT"

It's not surprising that it took a while for Baltimore CORE members to figure out the most effective ways to bring about change. They were volunteers with regular jobs who joined together in

Courtesy Hearst Corporation

Gwynn Oak continued to expand during the 1950s. Here, workers fix up one of the rides—a roller coaster, also known as a "racer-dip," April 1959.

A TRAGIC AUGUST 28TH

On the minds of some at CORE's first All Nations Day protest at Gwynn Oak in 1955 was a tragedy that had occurred a few days earlier in Mississippi. Emmett Till, a 14-year-old black teenager from Chicago, was visiting his uncle in Mississippi and allegedly whistled at a white woman. Her husband and brother-in-law kidnapped the boy in the early morning hours of August 28, 1955, tortured and killed him, and dumped his body in a river, where it was found three days later. News reports of his murder and funeral appeared in Baltimore newspapers on September 4, the day of the Gwynn Oak protest. Shocking photos of the brutalized body appeared later. Also shocking was the not-guilty verdict by an all-white jury in the trial of his killers. This tragedy strengthened the resolve of those determined to end Jim Crow.

their spare time to try to end discrimination. Most didn't have much experience organizing demonstrations. "People were making it up as they went," said John Roemer, age 23 and just out of college when he joined Baltimore CORE in 1961. Although local CORE members received some advice from the national CORE office in New York, most branches operated pretty much on their own.

Actually, everyone in the civil rights movement was "making it up as they went," figuring out along the way what worked and what didn't.

However, by the early 1960s, after years of protests that failed to change Gwynn Oak, Baltimore CORE began experimenting with different approaches, thanks to young, activist members who took leadership roles in the chapter. Among those new leaders were John Roemer and another recent college student, Charles Mason, along with a dynamic young social worker who took over as head of Baltimore CORE in 1961, Walter P. Carter. These CORE newcomers were open to trying some of the more daring tactics that had begun making headlines throughout the South during the late 1950s and into the early '60s, approaches that involved economic pressure, arrests, and loads of publicity.

These more effective tactics first rocked the civil rights world in a yearlong protest in Montgomery, Alabama, that began in late 1955, a few months after the first All Nations Day picketing at Gwynn Oak. The Montgomery protest introduced a new, young civil rights leader—Rev. Dr. Martin Luther King, Jr.—who quickly became a prime spokesperson in America for Gandhi's ideas. The protest strategies used in Montgomery and at other demonstrations that followed elsewhere in the South gradually made their way to Baltimore and would be put to good use at Gwynn Oak Amusement Park before too many more All Nations Days had passed.

"*We will match your capacity to inflict suffering with our capacity to endure suffering. . . . We will not hate you, but we cannot in all good conscience obey your unjust laws.*"

—Rev. Dr. Martin Luther King, Jr., *Stride Toward Freedom*, 1958

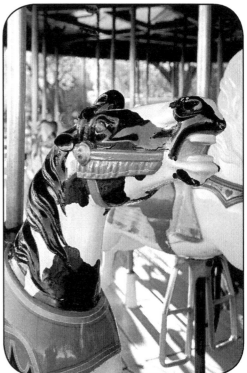

© James Singewald

TOUGH TACTICS
DOWN SOUTH

1955 to 1961

D URING THE FIRST FEW YEARS of the Gwynn Oak protests in Baltimore—from 1955 to 1961—activists in states farther south began using tactics that wound up changing the nature of civil rights protests everywhere, Baltimore included.

Leading the way was the Montgomery Bus Boycott. This protest began on December 5, 1955, in response to the arrest a few days earlier of Rosa Parks, who had refused to move to the back of a local bus in Montgomery, Alabama. This city's African American community was fed up with the daily humiliation of coping with a Jim Crow bus system and decided to boycott the buses until the transit company dropped its insulting segregation policies.

To head up the boycott effort, local leaders selected Rev. Dr. Martin Luther King, Jr., a 26-year-old newcomer to the city who had recently earned a doctorate in philosophy from Boston University. He had just started his first job, as the pastor of a Montgomery church.

Dr. King had never run a protest movement, but he knew about Gandhi's work in India and felt that nonviolent protest would be

The arrest of Rosa Parks in December 1955 sparked the Montgomery Bus Boycott. Here she is arrested again, February 1956, for taking part in the bus boycott.

AP Photo/Gene Herrick

a good way to oppose Jim Crow. Dr. King was a powerful speaker with a unique ability to inspire people and motivate them to take action. This was clear from the first speech he gave as boycott leader. After an amazingly successful opening day of the boycott, during which thousands of Montgomery's black citizens refused to ride the city's buses, Dr. King spoke to a huge crowd gathered in a local church for a nighttime rally. His job was to urge them to choose nonviolent protest, despite the anger they felt over years of discrimination. By describing the nonviolent strategy in terms of basic Christian teachings, he persuaded the pastors and church-goers in the crowd to give nonviolence a try.

As the boycott continued, people would gather for weekly meetings to discuss Gandhi's ideas and protest strategies. Dr. King called Gandhi's strategy "nonviolent resistance." The boycotters' commitment to nonviolence remained strong, even when they were harassed and arrested, or when segregationists bombed the homes of Dr. King and another leader.

Several Gandhi experts, impressed by the power of the boycott, visited Montgomery in February 1956 to discuss strategy with Dr. King and to help him learn more about Gandhi's techniques. These experts included Glenn Smiley, a white Methodist minister from Texas, and Bayard Rustin, one of the African Americans who had taken part in CORE's 1947 Journey of Reconciliation bus protest. Mr. Rustin had also walked the Ford's Theatre picket line in Baltimore in 1948. He soon became a regular, long-term advisor to Dr. King and was one of the chief organizers of the 1963 March on Washington for Jobs and Freedom.

Of course, a boycott was not a new idea. People had been staging boycotts for various reasons for years. For example, in 1933, Juanita Jackson Mitchell and other young Baltimoreans organized a boycott to pressure stores in black neighborhoods to hire black workers. (See chapter 2.) The Montgomery Bus Boycott stood out from earlier civil rights boycotts because it involved many more protestors, it lasted longer, and it earned much more news coverage. It also energized others who were battling Jim Crow around the country.

For 381 days, tens of thousands of Montgomery's African American citizens stayed off the buses. Many of them did a good deal of walking that year, both to get to work and to go shopping. Others managed to catch rides with a well-run carpool system set up by boycott leaders. As part of this carpool, more than a hundred black Montgomery residents volunteered to use their cars to pick up and drop off boycotters at various locations around the city. Some African American women who worked as housekeepers got rides to and from work with the white housewives who employed them. However, some of those white women made it clear that they drove their housekeepers to keep them safe, not to support the boycott.

Very few white Montgomery residents supported the boycott. Those who did were often harassed by other whites, as happened to librarian Juliette Morgan. Angry whites hurled rocks through her windows, insulted her, and tried to have her fired from her job because she dared to write a letter to the local newspaper pointing

Rev. Dr. Martin Luther King, Jr., with his wife, Coretta, and cheering supporters, after an Alabama judge found him guilty of leading the bus boycott.

AP Photo/Gene Herrick

out that the boycotters were following in the footsteps of Gandhi and of famous American author Henry David Thoreau.

This yearlong bus boycott inflicted significant economic pain on the bus company. African Americans had been its main customers. Before the boycott, blacks had taken from 30,000 to 40,000 bus rides a day. Without those customers, the bus company lost so much money that it had to shut down some bus lines and lay off workers. Local stores lost money, too, because without being able to ride buses, blacks had a hard time reaching stores to go shopping.

IN THE NEWS

News coverage of the boycott increased markedly after Dr. King and about a hundred others were arrested in early 1956. Most of those arrested were released fairly soon after paying bail, but the fact that they were willing to face arrest made the boycott newsworthy to reporters. Some arrests were for trumped-up traffic violations. Other protestors faced arrest simply for taking part in a boycott, which in most other parts of the country would not be considered a crime. Some boycotters turned themselves in voluntarily, after learning that the police were about to arrest them. They believed that unfair arrests would help, not hurt, the boycott. They were right. Reporters, always interested in events that are ground-breaking and dramatic, flocked to Montgomery.

Dr. King held press conferences several times a week to speak with all the reporters, American and foreign, who came to Montgomery. Thanks to these reporters, people across the country and around the world learned more about the unfairness of Jim Crow.

News coverage can definitely increase the effectiveness of a nonviolent protest and give it a better chance of achieving Gandhi's goal of changing people's attitudes. Dramatic news reports about the arrest and mistreatment of peaceful protestors can make people feel ashamed that such things could happen in their country. As Dr. King explained in the book he wrote about the Montgomery Bus Boycott, *Stride Toward Freedom*, "We will so appeal to your heart and conscience that we will win you in the process."

News coverage of the boycott had another benefit. It motivated people around the country to send money to help the boycott continue. Dr. King noted in his book that a large portion of the contributions came from churches, especially African American churches, and from branches of the NAACP around the country. Donations also came from individuals, both black and white. The National Council of Churches sent a financial contribution and a strong telegram of support. At that time, Rev. Dr. Eugene Carson Blake, a white Presbyterian minister, was the head of this council, which was made up of the major Protestant churches in the country. Dr. Blake would later play an important role in the 1963 protests that ended segregation at Gwynn Oak.

In addition to giving interviews to reporters, Dr. King was invited to give speeches in other cities and write articles about the boycott. These speeches and articles let more people learn about

GANDHI'S NEWS

Success "depends . . . on cultivation of public opinion and public support," Mohandas Gandhi wrote in 1922, when he became the leader of the effort to gain India its independence from Britain. He was a master at dealing with reporters. Before his famous Salt March of 1930, he sent bulletins to reporters around the world, several of whom followed along as he walked 240 miles from his home to a coastal city. There he boiled sea water to make salt. That was illegal. India's British rulers said only the British could make, sell, and collect tax on salt in India. Gandhi gave interviews to reporters during his twenty-four day march to the sea. Stories appeared nearly every day in the *New York Times*. More than 60,000 Indians followed his lead, made salt, and were arrested. Gandhi even gave interviews from jail. News stories won him followers around the world, including Martin Luther King, Jr., a college senior when Gandhi was assassinated in India in 1948.

nonviolent resistance. As James Farmer, one of CORE's founders, wrote later, "No longer did we have to explain nonviolence to people. Thanks to Martin Luther King, it was a household word. CORE was a beneficiary of the emergence of King."

The Montgomery Bus Boycott ended on December 20, 1956, thanks to another tactic in the protest line-up: the NAACP's legal team. NAACP lawyers had filed a court case on behalf of several African Americans who had been arrested in Montgomery for not going along with the city's Jim Crow bus-seating rules. The U.S. Supreme Court decided that those rules were illegal. From then on, African Americans could sit wherever they pleased on Montgomery buses.

This court victory didn't have much impact in other cities, however. In Baltimore, buses were already integrated. But in most areas in the Deep South, local buses were still segregated and remained so even after this 1956 Supreme Court decision.

Although the Montgomery Bus Boycott didn't end Jim Crow everywhere, it had a huge impact on civil rights activists. The boycott showed that the frustration of the African American community could be harnessed in a massive, effective protest. The boycott highlighted a powerful set of tactics that could be put to use elsewhere: nonviolent resistance, large numbers of protestors, focused economic pressure, a willingness to face arrest, and lots of news coverage. Baltimore CORE members would eventually employ such strategies at Gwynn Oak, but it took college students to help them learn how.

1960 STUDENT-LED SIT-INS

By the start of 1960, more than three years had gone by since the December 1956 Supreme Court victory ended the Montgomery Bus Boycott. That ruling had raised hopes that the federal government might now end other examples of Jim Crow. That hadn't happened. President Eisenhower did send Army troops to Arkansas in the fall of 1957 to escort and protect the African American students who integrated Little Rock's Central High School. But even that advance had a downside, when Little Rock officials closed the city's public high schools for the whole next school year to avoid having to integrate further.

During the latter part of the 1950s, activists in several cities organized local protests against Jim Crow, such as those at Gwynn Oak Amusement Park. But there had been no big, attention-grabbing demonstrations like the Montgomery boycott. The NAACP pursued court cases during those years, but there were few major victories on that front either. There had been some signs of progress in states on the northern rim of the South, including Maryland. By the spring of 1957, all but three of Maryland's counties had followed Baltimore's lead and had begun to end segregation in their public schools or were making plans to do so. But Baltimore's restaurants and department stores still practiced segregation, as did many of its businesses. In states farther

Students holding a sit-in at the Woolworth's lunch counter in Greensboro, North Carolina, February 1960.

© Bettmann/Corbis

South, Jim Crow continued to rule the schools and just about everything else. The pace of change was slow and frustrating.

In early 1960, North Carolina college students decided to speed things up. On Monday, February 1, 1960, four freshmen who attended an all-black North Carolina university held a lunch-counter sit-in at a Woolworth's variety store in Greensboro, North Carolina. Blacks could buy school supplies and other items in that store but were not allowed to eat at its lunch counter. When these four young men sat down at the lunch counter that day, the waitress refused to bring them the coffee and doughnuts they ordered. So they sat there until the store closed for the day. All week, additional students joined the sit-in. By week's end, more than 300 had participated, including some white students. Crowds of angry segregationists participated, too—by harassing and shouting insults at the protestors.

TV and newspaper reporters showed up and did stories on the sit-ins. Word spread to other college campuses. Nonviolent student-led sit-ins began to spring up elsewhere, first in other cities in North Carolina, then in South Carolina, Virginia, Tennessee, and Florida. In some cities, police arrested protesting students. In Nashville, more than seventy-five students were arrested during a sit-in demonstration on February 26. At the end of March, sit-ins were underway in thirteen states. By year's end, more than 50,000 people in over 100 cities had participated in lunch-counter protests. Police had arrested about 3,000 of the protestors.

These sit-ins were mainly student-run events, although the NAACP, CORE, and other organizations offered help and support. Dr. King joined students in October 1960 at a sit-in in Atlanta, Georgia. He was arrested and spent eight days in jail. By then, Dr. King was the head of a new organization of Southern ministers, the Southern Christian Leadership Conference. Through his speeches, writings, and protest activities, he had become a symbol to many Americans of the nonviolent approach to solving problems. His arrest sparked more news coverage for the sit-ins.

Sit-ins were not a new tactic. Others had done this before, including the founders of CORE who held their first sit-in in Chicago in 1942. Baltimore college students had staged sit-ins in the mid-1950s, as had activists in a few other cities. But those earlier sit-ins never received the nationwide news coverage that the 1960 Greensboro sit-ins did. By then, civil rights events were gaining more news coverage in general, partly as a result of the Supreme Court's 1954 school desegregation decision and the turmoil that ruling unleashed in many cities. The Montgomery Bus Boycott had also primed the news media to be on the lookout for new protests to cover. In addition, TV reporters were playing a bigger role in news coverage, bringing stirring images from protests right into people's living rooms. The 1960 sit-ins, with their dedicated, serious-minded students, made for good news stories.

All the news reports, along with the disruption the sit-ins caused at the stores, showed many store owners that sticking with Jim Crow might lead to what Gwynn Oak's owner feared: economic suicide. The Greensboro Woolworth's reportedly lost $200,000 worth of business during the sit-ins. In July 1960, that Woolworth's dropped Jim Crow. Soon, other lunch counters did, too.

The sit-ins showed the value of many of the same tactics that had proved effective in Montgomery: large numbers of nonviolent protestors, economic pressure, willingness to face arrest, lots of news coverage, plus a new element—marshalling the power of young people.

FREEDOM RIDES

Another protest tactic that had originated with Gandhi—mass arrests—earned headlines the next year, 1961, as part of a new CORE campaign that rolled through the South. This tactic would later make its way to Baltimore—and to Gwynn Oak. But first, CORE demonstrated how effective a mass arrest approach could be in its new bus-ride protest, launched in May 1961. This campaign was similar to the bus protest CORE had sponsored in 1947. (See chapter 3.) This time, CORE gave its bus project a much more dramatic name: Freedom Rides.

A Supreme Court case once again served as the focus for CORE's bus protest. The Freedom Rides were designed to test the impact of a 1960 NAACP Supreme Court victory, which outlawed segregation at restaurants in bus stations used by interstate buses. Many Southern bus stations refused to go along with this Supreme Court ruling, something CORE hoped to publicize through its Freedom Rides.

The Freedom Rides were supposed to last only two weeks and involve thirteen volunteers—seven blacks and six whites, mostly men, but a few women, too. However, the Freedom Rides quickly mushroomed into something much bigger, involved many more volunteers, and dominated the news for months.

The original plan was for the thirteen volunteers to undergo several days of nonviolent protest training in Washington. Then they would buy tickets on Greyhound and Trailways buses and were supposed to spend two weeks traveling by bus from Washington to New Orleans. Three reporters set out on the trip with the CORE volunteers to record what happened.

The journey began on May 4, 1961, and for a little more than a week things went fairly well. The Riders discovered that Jim Crow seating had pretty much ended on most of the interstate buses they traveled on through Virginia, North Carolina, South Carolina, and Georgia. CORE volunteers were usually not challenged for sitting wherever they liked. But it was a different story when they climbed off a bus and walked into a bus station. Shops, restaurants, and lunch counters in station waiting rooms refused to serve CORE's Riders. Some were arrested for trying to enter the shops. At the first stop in South Carolina, a group of local whites battered three Riders when they entered the town's Greyhound station. The worst injured, with sore ribs and cuts to his face, was John Lewis, a 21-year-old student who years later became a member of the U.S. Congress.

Worse violence greeted CORE volunteers when their buses rolled into Alabama. On Sunday, May 14, 1961—Mother's Day—a Greyhound bus carrying Freedom Riders reached the station in Anniston, Alabama. Mobs of segregationists, aided by the local police, attacked the bus, slashed its tires, and broke its windows. As it headed out of town, carloads of segregationists followed and attacked the bus when a flat tire forced it to stop. Someone in the mob tossed a firebomb through one of the broken windows. The Freedom Riders, gasping for breath as the bus filled up with smoke, managed to escape as the bus burst into flames.

That same day, Freedom Riders on a Trailways bus heading to Birmingham, Alabama, were attacked even before arriving. They were assaulted along the way by segregationists who had also

This Greyhound bus was carrying Freedom Riders when it was attacked in Anniston, Alabama, on May 14, 1961, by a mob of whites, who set the bus on fire while the CORE volunteers were still on board. Luckily, they managed to escape.

© Bettmann/Corbis

boarded the bus. A mob at the Birmingham bus station delivered additional beatings when the Freedom Riders got off the bus. One white Rider, James Peck, was beaten so badly that it took fifty-three stitches to close the wound on his head. He was a longtime civil rights activist, having been on CORE's earlier bus campaign in 1947. He had also been in Baltimore in 1958, taking part in All Nations Day picketing at Gwynn Oak.

Howard K. Smith, a CBS reporter who was in Birmingham that day, phoned in reports all that afternoon to CBS radio about the attacks on the Freedom Riders. CBS carried his eyewitness accounts live on CBS radio news, letting people across the country find out about the violence.

The segregationist mob seemed to realize that news stories would help the Freedom Riders. The mob delivered its blows quickly and then scattered, but a local news photographer managed to show up in time to take a photo of a beating. The attackers then turned on the cameraman, smashing his camera to the ground. Later, after the mob had gone, another photographer found the damaged camera. The film was still good. The next day, the *Birmingham Post-Herald* newspaper published a photo of the beating. It turned out that the victim wasn't a Freedom Rider but a local man who happened to be in the station and was set upon by the mob anyway.

The *New York Times, Washington Post,* and other newspapers also carried stories about the Alabama violence. Injured Freedom Riders gave interviews that were broadcast on TV news shows. Shocking photos appeared in newspapers across the nation and around the world, showing the burned-out bus and bloodied, battered Freedom Riders. These reports spread the word about the cause for which the Riders were risking their lives.

Other civil rights groups mobilized to keep the Freedom Rides going. Dr. King spoke at a rally in Montgomery, Alabama, after the beating of young people from Nashville who had decided to join the Freedom Rides. Hundreds more volunteers—blacks and whites—joined this traveling civil rights demonstration, riding on buses through the South during the summer of 1961. Some volunteers were members of a new student protest group formed after the North Carolina sit-ins, the Student Nonviolent Coordinating Committee (SNCC—pronounced "snick").

JAIL-NO-BAIL

With so many volunteers joining the Freedom Rides, many more people wound up being arrested. A lot of them chose a new tactic— "jail-no-bail"—that made their arrests much more troublesome for segregationist officials. Usually when civil rights protestors had been arrested, they paid bail, which let them get out of jail fairly quickly, as long as they promised to show up later for a court hearing. However, many Freedom Riders decided that instead of paying bail, they would stay in jail and would also refuse to pay a fine, so that they would have to serve out a prison sentence. By staying in jail, they hoped to overwhelm the local court and prison systems, as Gandhi's followers had done in India.

CORE volunteers had tried using jail-no-bail with sit-ins in Florida the previous year and in South Carolina during February 1961. Leaders of CORE encouraged protestors to choose jail-no-bail, when possible, for the Freedom Rides, too. In some cases, the sentences handed out to Freedom Riders were several months long. Officials in Mississippi found themselves having to deal with more than 300 Riders willing to fill up the state's prison cells.

James Farmer, CORE's national director, used the jail-no-bail strategy himself when he was arrested with other Freedom Riders in Jackson, Mississippi. He spent more than a month imprisoned in Mississippi, enduring the same tough conditions as other inmates at the state's dreaded Parchman Prison Farm, well known for its harsh treatment of prisoners. He noted later that it cost Mississippi hundreds of thousands of dollars to keep him and other Freedom Riders locked up for so long. He concluded, "We must make it increasingly expensive for the South to practice segregation."

Reports in newspapers and on TV about the vicious beatings and imprisonment of Freedom Riders made a strong impression

James Farmer, CORE's national director in 1961, helped design the Freedom Ride campaign and was a Freedom Rider himself, arrested in Jackson, Mississippi.

© Bettmann/Corbis

on top U.S. government officials. They realized that those news stories harmed the nation's image around the world. The U.S was engaged in a fierce competition with the Soviet Union, a Communist country. During that same summer of 1961, the Communists built a wall in Germany between East and West Berlin to force East Germans to live under Communism and prevent them from escaping to the democratic West. It would be hard to convince other nations that American democracy was better than Communism when people saw photos of peaceful American demonstrators being beaten and arrested.

At first, U.S. officials urged CORE to stop the Freedom Rides for a "cooling off period." CORE refused. "We had been cooling off for 100 years," said CORE's leader, James Farmer. "If we got any cooler we'd be in a deep freeze." That spurred President John F. Kennedy and his brother, Attorney General Robert Kennedy, to take decisive action. In September 1961, about four months after the Freedom Rides started, the federal government's Interstate Commerce Commission (ICC) issued strict new rules that it promised would be enforced, rules that ended segregation in all interstate buses and bus stations. Jim Crow was kicked out of train and airplane travel, too. By mid-1963, the Jim Crow era in interstate transportation had pretty much ended. One year later, in 1964, most Southern cities had banished segregation from their local buses, too.

EMBARRASSED INTO ACTION

The ICC's 1961 rules against Jim Crow travel were similar to ones it had already issued in 1955. The earlier rules came thanks to two young African American women: Sarah Keys Evans, arrested in 1952 at age 22 for not moving to the back of a bus in North Carolina, and her lawyer, Dovey Roundtree, who filed a complaint about the arrest with the ICC. In November 1955, the ICC said neither states nor bus companies could limit where blacks sit on interstate buses, but those rules were never enforced down South. It took the 1961 Freedom Rides to embarrass the government into finally taking firm action.

Sarah Keys Evans, a 22-year-old in the Women's Army Corps at the time of her 1952 bus arrest, achieved a 1955 victory at the ICC against Jim Crow seating on interstate buses.

However, Jim Crow was still in charge of many other aspects of daily life in the Deep South and in Baltimore, too. But clues for how to loosen Jim Crow's grip had been revealed in the successful Southern protests of 1955 to 1961: the Montgomery Bus Boycott, the North Carolina sit-ins, and the Freedom Rides. James Farmer summed up the secrets of protest success by noting that change came only "when the heat is on." He said CORE's goal would be "to continue to create crises like the Freedom Rides."

In the early 1960s, those change-producing crises reached Baltimore—and Gwynn Oak's merry-go-round—when Baltimore's own college students began to master the new tactics that had been so effective down South: economic pressure, mega publicity, huge protests, mass arrests, and topping it off, jail-no-bail.

"I shall continue to believe I am within my rights to expect equal treatment in public places for myself and all human beings."

—Mary Sue Welcome, from her article in the *Baltimore Afro-American*, July 16, 1960

© James Singewald

BALTIMORE STUDENTS
TAKE CHARGE

1959 to 1962

E ARLY VICTORIES FOLLOWED BY years of frustration—that was the story of the late 1950s for Baltimore civil rights activists. It was true for the local chapter of CORE and also for CIG, the student-run protest group that had been organized by Morgan State College students in 1955. Both CORE and the students did well in the early 1950s, integrating several Baltimore lunch counters. From 1955 to 1959, each group tackled new targets but failed to oust Jim Crow from most of them.

CORE's main targets in the late 1950s were Gwynn Oak Amusement Park and a chain of restaurants called the White Coffee Pot, a fitting name for a whites-only eatery. CIG focused on the segregated movie theater at Northwood Shopping Center, a short walk from the Morgan campus.

There had been some progress in Baltimore on other fronts during the late 1950s. Mondawmin, a new shopping center, had opened in northwest Baltimore, and all its stores were integrated except one, its White Coffee Pot. In addition, by 1959, many downtown movie theaters had voluntarily dropped Jim Crow, although some outlying movie theaters, such as the one near Morgan, remained segregated.

Hotels offered good news, too. One by one between 1957 and 1959, Baltimore hotels dropped Jim Crow. NAACP officials and others persuaded the hotels that it would be hard to entice national organizations to hold conventions in Baltimore if their black members couldn't find hotel rooms. Robert Watts explained that the NAACP joined forces with members of a largely white organization, Americans for Democratic Action, to "put pressure on the hotels . . . telling people not to stay at the hotels. Then one hotel opened [to blacks] and then we had everybody go there. Economic pressure was brought to bear and they all finally opened."

Despite these signs of progress, Jim Crow was still in control of much of the city. Downtown restaurants were segregated. So were department store restaurants.

But not for long.

CIG's luck changed in 1959. By then, protest had become a springtime tradition for CIG, most of whose members were Morgan students, with a few whites from other local colleges participating from time to time. Each spring, CIG organized several days of picketing at the Northwood Theatre. Each spring, this movie theater refused to change. Sometimes students also picketed other segregated businesses at the shopping center. Most of them refused to change, too.

The 1959 protest season turned out better. That year CIG students targeted the shopping center's Arundel Ice Cream store, right next door to the movie theater. Hundreds of students picketed or engaged in sit-ins at this ice cream parlor. On some days, as many as 400 students walked the picket line. To everyone's surprise, the store manager gave in and opened the shop to all. The take-home lesson: The more protestors—the more effective the demonstration. Maybe the manager realized that all those young picketers were potential ice cream lovers who could help him earn more money if he welcomed them as customers.

However, the manager of the shopping center's movie theater didn't reach the same conclusion. Nor did the manager of another

Baltimore police at the Arundel Ice Cream store where Morgan State College students scored a protest victory in March 1959.

Courtesy Afro-American Newspapers Archives

store at the shopping center that CIG targeted that year, a branch of the Hecht-May Company chain of department stores. Blacks could shop at that department store but were not allowed to eat at its Rooftop Restaurant. The next year—1960—CIG students found a way to win seats at the table.

TAKING CENTER STAGE

When it was time for CIG to plan its 1960 campaigns, events outside of Baltimore had changed the protest climate. Suddenly, sit-ins were the hot, new thing. Morgan students, of course, had been staging sit-ins since the mid-1950s. But in February 1960, North

Carolina college students had suddenly turned sit-ins into a national sensation with their Greensboro protest, which started a wave of sit-ins that was sweeping the country. (See chapter 5.)

Taking part in another CIG sit-in at Northwood Shopping Center was no longer just a Baltimore thing to do. "The civil rights movement was beginning to grow and more college students were becoming interested in working against social injustice," explained Joyce l. Dennison, a Morgan student in the early 1960s. The sense of being part of a spreading national movement may have spurred more Morgan students to turn out for CIG's spring-of-1960 protests. It may also explain why other civil rights groups in Baltimore encouraged CIG to take its protests to a new level. That helped the students master a new skill: grabbing the public's attention.

CIG's protests in March 1960 started with hundreds of students showing up at the Hecht-May's Rooftop Restaurant in Northwood Shopping Center. Students picketed and conducted sit-ins there for more than a week, staying at the store for as long as twelve hours a day. CORE members offered their support, as did other local groups. Some African American ministers joined the picket line, too. Five students were arrested. This massive protest disrupted business so much that the store manager refused to let students anywhere near the restaurant. No problem—they picketed outside.

The state's Commission on Interracial Problems and Relations tried to negotiate a solution, but failed. The store's owner went to court and filed a complaint against the protestors for causing the store to lose money. A judge ruled that only two students at a time could picket at the store.

The judge's order turned out to be a blessing in disguise. It helped the students make a bold, new move that brought them the kind of publicity that carried success along with it. The new approach also helped CIG earn the 1960 Hollander Award.

Before 1960, CIG protests hadn't received much news coverage. That changed because of advice from an Urban League official. On his own, without the students' knowledge, he had been con-

Courtesy Afro-American Newspapers Archives

Morgan students at a sit-in at the Hecht-May Company's Rooftop Restaurant in Northwood Shopping Center, March 1959.

ducting private talks with the Hecht-May department store owner in an effort to reach a settlement. This was something the Urban League was noted for, behind-the-scenes negotiations. The official urged the students to move their protests downtown, where the main branch store of the Hecht-May chain was located, along with the main stores of the city's other department stores. Actually, the Hecht-May owner supported the move downtown and had discussed it with the Urban League official. If the students picketed the main downtown branches of all four of the city's major department stores and persuaded the other three to change, then Hecht-May would change, too. Like the owners of Gwynn Oak, he feared economic suicide. If his were the only store to drop Jim Crow in its restaurant, he worried that his white customers would flee to his competitors.

At first the students rejected the idea of moving downtown, several miles from the Morgan campus. Students would have a hard time traveling back and forth. The NAACP came to the rescue by donating money to rent buses to take the students into town. The NAACP also provided bail money for the five students arrested at the shopping center. Robert Watts served as the students' lawyer and managed later to have the charges against them dropped.

The NAACP's Juanita Jackson Mitchell, who had started student activism in Baltimore back in the 1930s with her "Don't Buy Where You Can't Work" boycott (see chapter 2), was now the mother of one of CIG's student leaders, Clarence Mitchell, III. He had walked the picket line with her a few years earlier in one of CORE's White Coffee Pot restaurant protests. In 1960, she formed a "Mother's Committee" to support the students' department store campaign, as her mother had done for her in the 1930s. Mrs. Mitchell encouraged her three younger sons to join the picket line, too, something they had done often at other demonstrations.

On the last Saturday in March 1960, four buses paid for by the NAACP brought several hundred college students—and a few professors, too—from the Morgan campus to downtown Baltimore, one busload for each of the major department stores. The plan was for students to picket and have sit-ins at the stores' restaurants. Three stores refused to serve the students. But one store, Hochschild-Kohn, surprised everyone and served them. The students hadn't brought along much money and almost didn't have enough to buy anything to eat.

BIG NEWS

Taking the sit-ins into the heart of the city brought the students more TV and newspaper coverage than ever before. This was the Easter shopping season, when department stores counted on selling a lot and earning a lot. Disruptions caused by the demonstrations might cut into profits. That alone would attract reporters. In addition, the move downtown took place just as national press coverage was heating up on the sit-ins down South. Here was a chance for Baltimore reporters to be part of a big news story. Also newsworthy was the presence of hundreds of African American college students downtown, still a mainly white area. The seriousness of the students and their commitment to nonviolent protest sparked reporter interest. So did the signs the students carried, which urged America to live up to its ideals: "WE WANT FULL CITIZENSHIP," "WANTED—DEMOCRACY," and "INTEGRATE—MAKE AMERICA GREAT."

As a result of the news stories, churches and other groups in both the black and white communities began donating money to help the students keep the sit-ins going. CORE and other local groups offered their assistance. The YWCA passed an official resolution calling on all the stores to follow the lead of Hochschild-Kohn.

White Baltimoreans wrote letters to the stores urging an end to segregation. Some whites even canceled their charge accounts at stores that refused to change. Concerned customers visited store officials to tell them Jim Crow had to go. This white involvement added a new kind of economic suicide for store owners to worry about, the kind that would come from losing white customers who *didn't* like segregation.

It turned out that the owners of the Hecht-May store and the other hold-out store were waiting for the head of Hutzler's department store to make up his mind. Hutzler's was regarded as the city's dominant department store. Albert Hutzler, Jr., the store's president, had been out of town. When he returned, he met with Robert Watts, CIG student leaders, and Urban League officials. Mr. Hutzler agreed to drop Jim Crow. Then the other stores did, too.

Jim Crow, which the stores had embraced in varying ways for so many years, suddenly lost its appeal when it drove away some of their best customers. After only about three weeks of demonstrations, the students had won. They had shown the effectiveness of taking a bold approach.

TIME TO GIVE UP

Walter Sondheim, head of Baltimore's school board in 1954 when it voted to integrate the schools, was also a vice-president of Hochschild-Kohn, the first department store to give in during the 1960 sit-ins. For many years he had worked at this store, where his father was an executive, and had tried to get it to drop its Jim Crow rules. Gradually, some restrictions ended, but it took the 1960 sit-in to end the last one, the restaurant rule. "We decided this was the time to give up," he said. "It's hard for me to believe that I'm working for a company that had such insulting practices." As in 1954 when it took the Supreme Court to get Sondheim's school board to act, it took pressure from an outside source—the sit-ins—to make it seem less risky for this store to do the right thing.

HIGH SCHOOLERS PITCH IN

After the department store victory, CIG and CORE teamed up to organize sit-ins at more Baltimore restaurants, including the White Coffee Pot chain that CORE had been picketing for years. Students from two of the city's largely white colleges—Johns Hopkins and Goucher—began turning out in larger numbers for these protests. Robert Watts began negotiating with restaurant owners. By May, about a dozen restaurants had dropped Jim Crow, but many others remained segregated, including some of the city's fanciest.

CIG wanted to keep the sit-ins going during the summer of 1960 after college classes ended. Because there wouldn't be many college students in town to walk picket lines, CIG asked high school students to help.

Robert Bell was one of the teens CIG contacted. This future judge was finishing his junior year at Dunbar High School and had just been elected student council president. He agreed to recruit high school students for a sit-in at Hooper's, a big downtown restaurant. At age 16, he was old enough, according to Baltimore laws, to be arrested as an adult. He realized he would be arrested at the sit-in. "I was flattered that they asked me," he said. "I thought it was the right thing to do. I also knew that if I told my mother, she would not have allowed me to go." He didn't tell her until *after* his arrest. "She was pleased deep down, was terribly supportive once the deed was done, but I knew not to tell her in advance."

The sit-in took place in mid-June, on the first day of summer vacation. Robert Bell took a bus to the restaurant and joined eleven other students there. They spent the first hour picketing outside Hooper's. "A counter-demonstration developed," he said. "White folks began to gather. They were not quiet. They were threatening. The angry faces are something I'll never forget." He was glad when it was time to go inside for the sit-in. "The arrest was easy. The waitress asked us to leave. Eventually a police officer came and asked us to leave. There was no violence. It was like a discussion. 'Will you leave?' 'No, we won't.'"

After a brief hearing before a judge, the students were allowed to go home. The judge found them guilty of trespassing, fined them each ten dollars, but the fines were later dropped. The NAACP appealed their convictions and three of its best lawyers worked on the case: Thurgood Marshall, Juanita Jackson Mitchell, and Robert Watts. The appeal eventually reached the U.S. Supreme Court. But this appeal illustrates the limits of trying to defeat segregation through the courts. Court cases move so slowly and are so complex that it wasn't until three years later, in 1963, that the Supreme Court heard the case. It reached its decision in 1964—to send the case back to Maryland's Court of Appeals, which in April 1965 finally overturned the students' convictions. By then, Congress had passed a law kicking Jim Crow out of all the nation's restaurants, thanks in part to the sense of crisis created by direct-action sit-ins, like the ones going on in Baltimore during the summer of 1960.

A few weeks after Robert Bell was arrested, more high school students landed in jail during a Hooper's sit-in. Among those arrested was 16-year-old Mary Sue Welcome. Spending time in a jail cell, "sealed my decision to become a lawyer," said Ms. Welcome, whose sister was also at the protest, picketing outside Hooper's. "My mother knew that I was participating, but I think my mother didn't know I was going to be arrested. It was scary. We had heard about what was going on in the South, but all we received was verbal abuse. Nobody tried to harm us." Even so, spending three hours in a "dilapidated" jail cell was upsetting. "Every time I think of that place, I shudder," she wrote in an article for the July 16, 1960, issue of the *Afro-American*. Around midnight, the police let her mother, Verda Welcome, a member of the Maryland legislature, pay her daughter's bail and take her home.

The Welcomes, mother and daughter, continued to participate in civil rights demonstrations, including ones at Gwynn Oak. But Robert Bell decided, "That was it for me as far as protest. The nonviolent strategy was valuable, but I realized it was not for everybody. I did not believe I had the temperament to do it." The hecklers at Hooper's alarmed him. He wasn't sure what he might

A protestor is arrested in November 1961 at Hooper's Restaurant, where Mary Sue Welcome and Robert Bell were arrested in June 1960.

AP Photo/William A. Smith

Here's how 16-year-old Mary Sue Welcome described her 1960 sit-in arrest in an essay she wrote for the July 16, 1960, issue of the *Afro-American*: "We are trying to do our bit to help release our country from the ugliness resulting from segregation and discrimination which ignore one's dignity. Personally, I am willing to do anything to accomplish this goal, even if it means being arrested. . . . I had only done what others around me were doing—asking to be served food. Yet, because I happened to have pigmentation in my skin, I was also breaking the law. This I cannot understand. God saw fit to make people with various colors, the same as he did plants and animals. Yet, I am penalized for what God did."

Mary Sue Welcome, Christmas Day, 1960.

do if a heckler attacked him. "That's when my resolve not to do it again came into being. You had to subject yourself to a lot. You just had to take it. I didn't want to be the one who would mess it up for everyone else."

FREEDOM RIDES, BALTIMORE STYLE

Restaurant sit-ins continued in Baltimore for the next two years, as CIG and CORE kept working together. By the fall of 1961, the protests had moved outside of Baltimore to restaurants located along Route 40, the main highway at the time from Washington, D.C., past Baltimore and on to Delaware. There had been news reports of African diplomats being turned away from restaurants on Route 40. These stories further embarrassed the U.S. government when its image in the world was already tarnished by the beatings of Freedom Riders in Alabama. Government officials tried to persuade Route 40 restaurant owners to drop Jim Crow, but they refused. So in the fall of 1961, CORE and CIG joined forces to bring sit-ins to Route 40. They called these sit-ins Freedom Rides, in honor of CORE's Southern bus campaign, which was nearing its end.

The Route 40 campaign led to more opportunities to learn new protest techniques, for both CORE and CIG. One important new skill that they mastered was broadening their pool of protestors. They did this by reaching out to student protest groups at colleges in Washington, Philadelphia, New York, and other cities. CORE's national office helped in making these connections. Hundreds of college students—white and black—from up and down the East coast traveled to Maryland on weekends during the fall of 1961 and into 1962, to join Baltimore students on picket lines. The out-of-towners not only increased the size of the demonstrations. They also showed that this wasn't just a local problem. It was an issue of national importance. CORE would later use many of these contacts with student groups to recruit protestors for Gwynn Oak.

However, in November 1961, the Route 40 Freedom Rides hit a snag. Maryland's Commission on Interracial Problems and Relations tried to negotiate a settlement with the restaurant owners. It obtained a promise from about half of the restaurants along Route 40 that they would drop Jim Crow in two weeks if protestors canceled a huge Freedom Ride planned for mid-November. CORE agreed to stop the protest. So did the NAACP, which was providing legal support for the protestors.

But nobody asked CIG's student leaders, including Clarence Logan, then the head of CIG. The students were furious about ending the sit-ins before *all* Route 40 restaurants dropped Jim Crow.

Those calling for a halt to the sit-ins—the NAACP, Urban League, and even some CORE officials—thought that headline-grabbing sit-ins might discourage local lawmakers from voting for laws that would make Jim Crow illegal at *all* restaurants and hotels. Since the mid-1950s, civil rights supporters in Baltimore had been working hard to persuade Baltimore's City Council and

Maryland's legislature to enact such laws. Year after year, the laws failed to pass. The state's Restaurant Association had even come out in favor of a statewide law, realizing that sooner or later segregation would be outlawed and that it would be better if all restaurants in the state had to make the change at the same time. If sit-ins continued, some people feared the Restaurant Association might stop backing the bill.

The students were in no mood to "cool it," especially given the advice they had heard from national civil rights leaders that summer at a conference that CIG and SNCC had organized in Baltimore. National civil rights leaders attended the conference, including CORE's national director, James Farmer, who stressed to the students the need to keep putting economic pressure on segregated businesses.

Rev. Dr. Martin Luther King, Jr., also spoke at this 1961 conference, telling the students, "To those who say cool off, we must say we cannot cool off in our determination to obtain our constitutional rights. Those who should cool off are those who are hot with hatred and violence." He urged the students to keep protesting, to "sit-in, wade-in, walk-in and read-in" until freedom "is a reality for all Americans." Dr. King praised the sit-ins down South, noting, "It would have taken fifteen years to integrate lunch counters through court action."

Dr. King also supported the passage of anti–Jim Crow laws. Otherwise, a restaurant might drop Jim Crow one day and bring it back the next. The question was: How to persuade lawmakers to pass such laws?

The students' answer: More demonstrations. They organized a new round of protests using the tactic that had worked so well for them in their department store victories—moving into the heart of Baltimore. Every Saturday from mid-November to mid-December in 1961, CIG had about 300 to 400 students protesting at more than fifty restaurants in Baltimore, including at Hooper's. Police arrested dozens of students.

CORE quickly realized that the students had made the right decision. CORE began supporting the students' efforts, especially

Courtesy Hearst Corporation

Hundreds of college students from New York, Washington, and Philadelphia joined Baltimore students in demonstrations at Baltimore restaurants, defying requests to "cool it," Saturday, November 11, 1961.

after it became clear that many of the Route 40 restaurants that had promised to integrate weren't doing so. In mid-December, CORE teamed up with CIG to launch a huge Freedom Ride that hit all Jim Crow restaurants on Route 40, from Baltimore to Delaware. More than 600 students took part.

After that, CORE and CIG worked together for more than a year to stage restaurant protests most weekends. The demonstrations occurred either in Baltimore, on Route 40, or on the Eastern Shore, a southern section of Maryland that was more like the Deep South than Baltimore. Protestors who ventured into the Eastern Shore faced angry mobs that were more threatening than the name-calling crowds in Baltimore. CORE also organized protests in the western Maryland city of Westminster. The protests received good press coverage. Several restaurants dropped Jim Crow.

Only a small percentage of demonstrators at these sit-ins were arrested. Most picketed outside the restaurants. Of those who entered a restaurant to stage a sit-in, many left when asked to do so. The organizers felt that a few arrests were enough to have an impact. However, Julius Hobson, a leader of the Washington, D.C., chapter of CORE, criticized the low-arrest approach, complaining that protestors would need to fill the jails to really have an impact. Baltimore activists weren't quite ready yet for a fill-the-jails approach.

NEW LEADERS

"We had demonstrations just about every Saturday during those years," said Charles Mason. "Every week was getting ready for the weekend coming up." CORE volunteers like Charles Mason generally made the arrangements for the protests. But most of the

Courtesy Hearst Corporation

The picket line at a Cambridge, Maryland, ice cream shop, February 1962.

demonstrators were students, although members of CORE and the NAACP were often on the picket lines, too, along with some of Baltimore's African American preachers.

The restaurant campaign provided another chance for Baltimore's civil rights groups to put differences aside and work together. When students needed help, the NAACP was there with lawyers and bail money. Rev. Marion C. Bascom noted that many black churches also provided bail and were staging areas for buses that took demonstrators to the restaurants.

"CORE and CIG were getting a lot of attention for these direct action tactics," said CORE volunteer John Roemer. "It made the NAACP look old-fashioned. But while we pooh-poohed their legal tactics, we were not ashamed to go to the NAACP for bail money. We didn't have any money. Walter Carter was a master at persuading them to support us even when they were kind of annoyed at what we were doing."

Walter P. Carter became chairman of Baltimore CORE in 1961. He, John Roemer, and Charles Mason were part of a new wave of Baltimore CORE members who shared the college students' impatient eagerness for change. They weren't far removed from college themselves. Charles Mason and John Roemer, both in their early twenties, had recently been college students. Walter Carter, in his late thirties, was back in school, studying part-time for a graduate degree in social work at Howard University in Washington, D.C., while also working as a social worker in Baltimore. Mr. Carter grew up in North Carolina and while in college there, he helped register blacks to vote, a dangerous thing for a young African American to do down South. He was inspired to join CORE in the spring of 1961 after seeing a shocking news photo of the bloody, battered face of a CORE Freedom Rider who had been attacked in Alabama. He became friends with another Howard student, Stokely Carmichael, who had been a Freedom Rider in Mississippi and was a leader of SNCC, the new national student protest group that had formed in 1960. Their friendship came in handy when Mr. Carter began organizing Route 40 sit-ins, making it easy for him to get SNCC's help in rounding up student participants.

These CORE newcomers had regular jobs, but devoted their evenings and weekends to plan and take part in protests. "Nobody got paid. In fact, we were spending our own money organizing demonstrations," said Charles Mason, who was working at that time as a clerk at the headquarters of the Social Security Administration, located not far from Gwynn Oak.

John Roemer, a high school teacher, grew up in a Baltimore suburb where he attended all-white schools. "All my time growing up, I had been an extreme right wing conservative," he said. He didn't become a civil rights supporter until his last year of college at Princeton, when a history course challenged him to think about what equal rights really meant. "I had no contact with black people before, but it struck me that America should live up to its promises," he noted. After earning a teaching degree at Harvard, he returned to Maryland and went "down to the office of the *Afro-American* newspaper and asked how to join the civil rights movement. They sent me to the office of CORE." It was nothing fancy—a small, basement room in a row house. The men he met there were glad to have his help. Soon he was organizing restaurant sit-ins. That created tension with his father, the restaurant manager at Hutzler's, the department store that was among the last to drop Jim Crow.

These new CORE volunteers were willing to try some edgy tactics, such as the publicity-grabber they cooked up while driving back from a protest on the Eastern Shore. On their car radio, they heard that Baltimore's mayor and the state's governor were about to meet at the still-segregated Hooper's restaurant. Figuring that such a meeting would attract reporters, John Roemer suggested that they drive straight to Hooper's and do a sit-in, using insider information about Hooper's that he knew because his father used to work there. He told the others in the car, "I know that they keep the door open in the back for the help. You guys go to the front door. Walter and I will go around to the back door."

When they reached Hooper's, "Sure enough, Walter and I sauntered in the kitchen door and sat down," Mr. Roemer recalled. "The waitress said, 'I'm sorry we don't serve Negroes.' Our standard response was, 'Well, we don't eat them. We'd rather have a sandwich.' They called the cops to throw us out. The cops get there just as the governor and mayor walked in. Perfect timing. It got reported on the news. That's the kind of stuff we tried to do. What we were trying to do was stir up such a furor that there would be a call for laws against Jim Crow to pass."

A LAW AT LAST

A Public Accommodations Law was approved finally by the Baltimore City Council on June 4, 1962. It made Jim Crow illegal in the city's hotels and restaurants. The relentless sit-ins and protests had played a big part in bringing about this victory. Equally important in getting the law passed were the many years of lobbying—letter writing, testifying at hearings, negotiating with officials—by NAACP and Urban League officials, religious leaders, labor leaders, human rights commissioners, members of civil liberties and peace groups, as well as others sympathetic to the cause.

Also creating a climate for change that led to passage of the law were the news reports of protests going on throughout the country. Economic pressure helped, too. As CORE's John Roemer noted, "Nobody wants to go to a restaurant if they see demonstrators outside." Another kind of economic pressure made an impact, when national groups threatened not to hold conventions in Baltimore because it still had segregated businesses.

The African American community's growing voting power played a big part in the passage of this new law. NAACP voter registration drives had steadily increased the number of black voters. Religious leaders and groups like the League of Women Voters aided in these efforts. In 1960, CIG students helped, too, by going door to door and signing up African American voters. That year's registration campaign brought in nearly 20,000 new black voters, who had a major effect on that fall's presidential election. President Kennedy probably would not have won Maryland in the 1960 election without the support of Baltimore's black voters.

Courtesy Afro-American Newspapers Archives

NAACP and CIG picketers at the Lord Baltimore Hotel in March 1962 urge the Child Welfare League not to hold conventions in Baltimore until the city has a Public Accommodations Law.

1962 SCORECARD

Some advances in Maryland since 1955.

Newly Integrated. Bathrooms at many firehouses; phone company telephone operators; offices of some banks and insurance companies; Baltimore office of the Department of Motor Vehicles; Baltimore Bar Association; hotels; restaurants; meter maids; Boy Scouts (Girls Scouts had integrated earlier); most downtown movie theaters.

Some "Firsts." 1956—first blacks licensed as master plumbers. 1957— first black judge on a state court; 1958—first interracial summer camp for kids, run by the YWCA at Druid Hill Park; 1962—first black superintendent of a branch post office; first black president of a local of the United Steelworkers union; first black student admitted to Johns Hopkins Medical School.

Local elected officials heard the message from that presidential election—the power of Baltimore's African American voters. That helped turn more politicians into supporters of the Public Accommodations bill. No doubt, this was because many of them felt it was the right thing to do, but it was also becoming clear that supporting the bill would be important for winning re-election. CIG students helped reinforce that message by picketing in support of the bill at City Hall in the spring of 1960. A few months later, in August 1960, about two dozen CIG students delivered the same message to lawmakers in the U.S. Congress. They walked all the way from Baltimore to Washington—about forty miles—to hold a protest demonstration in the Rotunda of the U.S. Capitol Building. There they joined about 300 other CIG members, mostly high school students, who had traveled to Washington by bus.

However, Baltimore's new 1962 Public Accommodations Law didn't cover movie theaters. The theater near the Morgan campus was as segregated as ever. It would be up to Morgan students to figure out how to force that theater to change. In the process, they introduced Baltimore to the new protest tactic that would be absolutely essential to achieving victory the following year at Gwynn Oak.

"These students . . . have inspired us all, and made us realize that . . . the day of the gradualist is at an end."

—Editorial, *Baltimore Afro-American*, February 23, 1963

© James Singewald

MASS ARRESTS
REACH BALTIMORE
1963

A LTHOUGH BALTIMORE'S NEW 1962 Public Accommoda-tions Law didn't cover movie theaters, most theaters in the city had already dropped Jim Crow by then. But one had not—the movie theater in the Northwood Shopping Center, the one that Morgan State College students and their protest group, CIG, had been trying to integrate since the mid-1950s.

By the start of 1963, that theater was the only Jim Crow busi-ness left in the Northwood Shopping Center, which was right down the street from the Morgan campus. All the years of student picketing at that shopping plaza had made an impression on its other stores, and one by one they had ended their segregation pol-icies. Now, 100 years after Lincoln issued the Emancipation Proc-lamation, CIG's student leaders decided it was long past time for that theater to end its insulting whites-only policy.

When CIG students began planning their 1963 protests at the theater, the group's faculty advisor, Morgan history professor Au-gust Meier, suggested using an extreme tactic—mass arrests. He described how effective it had been in CORE's Freedom Rides down South and in protests in several other cities. The students decided to give it a try.

But in order for a mass arrest approach to work, CIG's leaders needed more demonstrators than usual. They came up with a clever strategy to broaden their base at Morgan by reaching out to a group of students who hadn't played a big role in past protests— the "popular" crowd. CIG persuaded some of Morgan's top athletes, the school's student council president, and even the winner of that year's "Miss Morgan" contest to take part in the first demonstration. If these student leaders joined the picket line, maybe other students would, too.

On the first day of the protest—Friday, February 15, 1963—fifty students picketed outside Northwood Theatre. About twenty-

Courtesy Hearst Corporation

Students, mostly from Morgan State College, picket Northwood Theatre, February 1963.

five students were arrested when they entered the theater lobby. Among the arrested was "Miss Morgan." The students spent the night in jail. They were released the next day without having to pay bail, but with a trial scheduled for later. Over the weekend, more students joined the picketing. About forty more landed in jail. Word of the arrests spread across campus.

On Monday afternoon, more than 500 students attended a meeting on the Morgan campus to learn about the protests. This huge turnout showed that the popular-crowd strategy was working. Rev. Marion C. Bascom, another CIG advisor, urged the students to "fill the jails," as Gandhi's followers had done. At that night's demonstration, 300 students picketed the theater and about 150 ended up in jail.

JAIL-NO-BAIL

The demonstration then took a more serious turn and shifted to a "jail-no-bail" event. That happened totally by accident when a judge came up with a plan that he thought would end the protest. He announced that students arrested on Monday couldn't be released until they each paid $500 in bail and a $100 fine. The students didn't have that much cash. Nor did CIG. To free all the students would cost more than $90,000. That was too much money to raise in a hurry. The students had no choice but to stay in jail.

However, the judge's plan backfired. Making bail so expensive didn't stop students from joining the protests. On the contrary, evening after evening, more of them landed in jail, including some from two other Baltimore colleges, Johns Hopkins and Goucher. In addition to those arrested, hundreds of others walked the picket line each night. Joining the students were a few Goucher professors and also some members of CORE, including a local postal worker, William Moore, who two months later would gain national attention when he was murdered during an unusual protest in Alabama.

Courtesy Afro-American Newspapers Archives

So many students were arrested at Northwood Theatre in February 1963 that police ran a shuttle of police vans from the theater to the stationhouse.

As hundreds of students languished in Baltimore jail cells, Juanita Jackson Mitchell joined a line of picketers marching in front of City Hall to show support for the jailed students and to protest the high bail the judge had set. Picketing with her were members of the postal workers union and students from local colleges.

Although the jail-no-bail strategy would be the key to the protest's success, it wasn't so wonderful for the students stuck in crowded, grimy cells. Some of those arrested early in the demonstration thought they would spend a few hours in jail and then get out. They didn't know why that hadn't happened because it was hard for student leaders on the outside to contact jailed students to let them know what was going on. (This was long before the age of cell phones and text messaging.) "We have no papers, no radio, or any way of knowing what's going on," said Germane Denneker, a jailed student who spoke with an *Afro-American* reporter who entered the jail to interview students. She added, "Tell them we are determined to stick it out."

A SPREADING CRISIS

By filling the jails, the students had created an enormous problem for the city, exactly what James Farmer, CORE's national director, meant when he told protestors to "continue to create crises." The arrests had overwhelmed Baltimore's jail and court systems. The city jail's regular prisoners were threatening to stage their own protest inside the jail because they were fed up with overcrowded cells caused by the sudden influx of student protestors, especially in the women's section. The regular inmates were also annoyed about special privileges that some student prisoners received, such as being given extra milk and textbooks.

Back at Northwood Shopping Center, where students continued to picket the movie theater each night, other store owners

Joyce I. Dennison (left), a Morgan student, and Harriet Cohen, a Goucher student, studying in jail after being arrested during the Northwood Theatre protests, February 1963.

AP Photo

DOING HER PART

"The first night I was in shock," said Joyce I. Dennison, a Morgan sophomore who spent three nights in jail during the Northwood Theatre protests. Then it became "a new adventure. I was scared, bored, but also excited. I was aware of protests going on down South. We knew there were plenty of battles to be fought, plenty of soldiers that were needed. We felt a part of that. Students on the outside covered for the students in jail. If a parent called the dorm, they'd say, 'Oh, she's at the library.' My mother didn't know I was there until my oldest sister saw a picture of me in jail in *Jet* magazine and called my mother." After getting out of jail, she concentrated on studying. "My mother said, 'You are the first in our family to go to college. We expect you to graduate,'" said Ms. Dennison, who after graduating became a teacher and later joined the Army.

---

were feeling overwhelmed. They had already dropped Jim Crow, but the hundreds of protestors at the theater were driving away *their* customers, too. Some shoppers brought coffee to the protestors and joined the picket line. A less-supportive crowd also showed up—segregationists who harassed the protestors. "The crowd would spit on you, attempt to throw hot coffee on you," said Joyce I. Dennison, one of the students who was arrested. "The police tried to keep the two groups apart, the demonstrators and the agitators."

Adding to the sense of crisis were reports on TV and in newspapers about the dreadful conditions that the students faced in overcrowded jail cells. Clarence Logan, a student leader in CIG, had become savvy about dealing with the press. He had taken part in earlier restaurant protests and had learned from those experiences how to obtain the best press coverage. For example, it was important to make sure that students were arrested before 8:00 or 9:00 P.M. so there would be enough time for reports about the arrests to make it onto that evening's late-night TV news programs. That would also give newspapers time to include stories in the next morning's editions. Not only did local reporters show up, but national ones did, too, including the *New York Times* and CBS-TV's famous newsman, Walter Cronkite.

AN EMBARRASSED CITY

The situation was a huge embarrassment for the city's mayor, Philip Goodman. He faced a primary election in two weeks. On Tuesday, the fifth day of the protest, he began negotiation sessions in his office to try to end the crisis. Participating in the negotiations were the theater's management, CIG student leaders, and the president of Morgan State College, along with Morgan professor August Meier, Robert Watts, and others.

At the second negotiation session on Wednesday, the theater management offered to start discussing possibly integrating five weeks later if CIG would stop picketing the theater. Absolutely not, said CIG's leaders. That evening, the students showed their

Four Morgan students flash the "V" for victory sign at Northwood Theatre on its first non–Jim Crow day, February 22, 1963.

AP Photo/William A. Smith

DISSING THE DUKE

Johns Hopkins was a largely white college in the early 1960s, having admitted a total of only thirty-one black undergraduates from 1944 to 1964. In 1953, when Rev. Chester Wickwire became a chaplain at Hopkins, he challenged students to take an interest in civil rights. He became friends with Baltimore's black leaders and also held interracial concerts on campus, including one with famous jazz band leader Duke Ellington in February 1960. On concert day, thirty white and five black Hopkins students held a sit-in at a segregated restaurant near the campus. After the concert, Rev. Wickwire took Duke Ellington to the restaurant. It refused to serve them. That led to more picketing. A fire closed the restaurant for a while, but the next year Hopkins students picketed there again—and joined sit-ins organized by CIG.

---

determination to keep up the pressure when about 500 demonstrators walked the picket line. Seventy-four were arrested.

By Thursday morning, February 21, Baltimore jails were brimming with nearly 350 young people. More than 1,500 people had taken part in the protest so far. There were rumors that hundreds of out-of-town college students from as far away as Boston would travel to Baltimore, eager to fill the city's jails even more. Clearly the crisis would continue until the Northwood Theatre did what most other movie theaters in Baltimore had already done—open their doors to everyone.

Finally, on Thursday, February 21, the Northwood Theatre management gave in. The students won. That afternoon the mayor announced that the theater would drop its Jim Crow rules the next day. Students left jail, without having to pay the huge bail fees. Later, all arrest charges against them were dropped.

A relieved mayor announced, "I am gratified that this situation has been alleviated since it has been giving our city and its people a bad reputation." He won his primary election, but he lost the general election for mayor that fall when voters brought back former mayor and longtime civil rights supporter Theodore McKeldin.

Professor August Meier, in an account he wrote about the Northwood campaign, said that the theater's "management appeared on television to say it was happy to join the ranks of progressive businessmen in northeastern Baltimore." Of course, the theater could have changed on its own at any time. But it didn't until it was forced to change, after students found just the right kind of pressure to exert. CORE's leaders had paid close attention to what the students had done and were ready now to apply some serious pressure of their own at Gwynn Oak.

"I believe in nonviolence as a tactic. I saw from Gandhi what could be done with it. But I would never let anyone come up to me on the street and spit in my face if it wasn't serving that purpose, of being a tactic in a demonstration. As a tactic, I could do it."

—Charles Mason, from a March 2010 interview

© James Singewald

TURNING UP
THE HEAT
AT GWYNN OAK

1962

B Y THE TIME CORE was ready to plan its 1962 Gwynn Oak protests, "Everyone was tired of doing the same thing without getting any results," said Charles Mason. He and other new members of Baltimore CORE were ready to try something different. In 1962, the Baltimore protest scene had changed dramatically from the days of the first picketing at Gwynn Oak back in 1955. A more assertive protest style had blown into town in 1960, with the in-your-face, student-led restaurant sit-ins.

Not only had those sit-ins led to the 1962 law that ended Jim Crow's reign in the city's restaurants and hotels, but they also let the CORE members who helped with the sit-ins gain valuable experience in setting up demonstrations that got results. During 1962 and on into 1963, CORE continued to team up with CIG students to hold restaurant sit-ins throughout Maryland. CORE paused, however, during the summer of 1962 to apply some of its newly-learned strategies to that year's Gwynn Oak campaign.

Walter P. Carter, chairman of Baltimore CORE from 1961 to 1963.

"The glory of being in Baltimore CORE was that you got to meet Walter Carter, who was chairman at the time," said John Roemer. As a young newcomer to CORE in his early 20s, Mr. Roemer looked up to 39-year-old Walter P. Carter as a mentor. "People were drawn to Walter Carter," said Mr. Roemer. "He was funny, serious, interested in jazz and all kinds of things. He was deeply committed. He taught me how to think tactically, how to tactically bring great pressure on people so that you could compel them to do the right thing." CORE members held weekly strategy sessions, "like a sensitivity session," Walter Carter explained to a *Sun* reporter. "This chapter had heart. . . . We'd thrash out philosophy. When we took a thing on the street, it was well-organized."

Like Charles Mason, John Roemer was also glad to try different approaches. "I was never much interested in carrying placards and going to rallies," he said. The new strategy that CORE volunteers used at Gwynn Oak in 1962 involved two features they had learned from the sit-ins: the importance of rounding up news coverage and of inflicting economic pain.

A *NO* NATIONS FESTIVAL

The economic pressure that CORE aimed at Gwynn Oak in 1962 involved a special kind of boycott that focused on one of the park's most popular features. CORE set out to persuade foreign embassies to boycott that year's All Nations Day Festival by not sending any representatives to the event—no costumed dancers, no native handcrafts, and no tasty ethnic dishes. Turning Gwynn Oak's big money-maker into a *No* Nations Festival would not only cause financial hardship for the park, but it would also cut into the publicity bounce Gwynn Oak usually received from positive news stories about the festival. If news outlets reported on a fizzled festival, that would remind people that Gwynn Oak was sticking with segregation at a time when quite a few Baltimoreans were adjusting well to the recently passed law that integrated the city's restaurants and hotels. Negative news about Gwynn Oak might make some customers think twice before lining up to buy tickets at this Jim Crow hold-out.

John Roemer, one of the architects of the *No* Nations boycott, had an unusual connection to Gwynn Oak. At that time, he was a teacher at the Friends School, a Baltimore private school. One of his seventh grade students was the son of James F. Price, co-owner of Gwynn Oak. As might be expected, a certain amount of friction had developed between Mr. Price and this young, activist teacher.

It took a bit of clever maneuvering on Mr. Roemer's part to persuade foreign embassies not to participate in the festival. CORE volunteers had tried doing this several years earlier without much success. This time, Mr. Roemer used hardball tactics. "I contacted all the embassies that participated and asked them to withdraw from All Nations Day," he recalled. "They rejected my request on the grounds that they couldn't interfere in domestic American politics. So I said, 'OK, I'll fix this.'" He set out to provoke Gwynn Oak's guards into having him arrested.

On August 25, a week before the All Nations Day Festival, CORE staged an earlier-than-usual demonstration at the park. Instead of picketing, John Roemer and Walter Carter walked into the park to try to buy tickets. They refused to leave when asked to do so, which led to their being arrested for violating the state's Trespass Law. This law said that if someone trespassed—entered

SPEEDY SUCCESS

"I belong to the human race," said Laurence Henry, a Howard University student who was answering the question—"What race do you belong to?"—asked by a guard at another segregated Maryland amusement park, Glen Echo, near Washington, D.C. This was on June 30, 1960, the first day of protests there, when more than sixty people picketed and five were arrested trying to ride Glen Echo's merry-go-round. Demonstrations continued all summer. By the time the park re-opened the next summer, Glen Echo had dropped Jim Crow. This speedy victory came in part from the nonstop picketing the summer before, the threat of new protests, and a boycott by the local recreation department, which stopped using the park's pool for swimming lessons.

a private business and refused to leave if asked to do so by the owner—that person could be arrested. This law had been used by restaurant owners to arrest people at all the sit-ins, too.

CORE let reporters know in advance about the demonstration so they could be there to describe what happened. "We were on friendly terms with most of the local reporters," explained Charles Mason. "Most of them were very sympathetic. A lot were just out of college or were still college students and were more agreeable to the changes that were happening in the country." Stories that reporters wrote about the August 25 demonstration played a big role in setting the stage for the *No* Nations Festival.

Those news reports explained that not only had Walter Carter and John Roemer been arrested, but that Gwynn Oak's private security guards had roughed up Mr. Roemer. Both men refused to pay bail and had to spend the night in jail. They would be released the next day and a trial would be set for later. Reporters added that CORE wasn't the only group picketing that day. After the arrest of the CORE leaders, a few picketers arrived to show *support* for Gwynn Oak's Jim Crow policy. These picketers were members of a new segregationist group—Fighting American Nationalists (F.A.N.).

The *Sun*'s article on the demonstration also contained an important announcement from CORE's "publicity chairman." CORE had become media-savvy and one volunteer, Lloyd Taylor, served as its spokesperson to the press. He announced that officials at the Indian Embassy had told CORE that the embassy would pull out of All Nations Day if there was evidence of Gwynn Oak discriminating against African Americans. The *Sun* news story about the arrests could be the kind of proof that the Indian diplomats needed. CORE sent them a copy of the article.

Mr. Roemer followed up with a phone call to Indian officials, telling them, "You are the biggest democracy in the world. How can you tolerate this?" His phone call succeeded. India withdrew from All Nations Day. "Then I called up other embassies," Mr. Roemer recalled. He told those other embassy officials, "India withdrew. Are you going to be there?"

The NAACP and students from CIG joined in the boycott effort by sending telegrams to embassies urging them to stay away from the festival. The strategy worked. All six embassies that had been invited to the festival that year refused to participate.

The next Sunday, the day of the 1962 All Nations Day Festival, no representatives of foreign embassies showed up at Gwynn Oak. But Walter Carter, John Roemer, and about eighteen other CORE volunteers were there, picketing and handing out leaflets that reinforced the economic message the boycott was making. The leaflets said, "Integration is good business."

About a dozen teenaged members of the segregationist group F.A.N. showed up at Gwynn Oak, too. Wearing F.A.N. armbands, they set up a picket line, but on a different section of the street than the CORE volunteers. A leader of F.A.N. handed out leaflets that described some of the organization's goals, which included establishing a "white man's party" and sending blacks back to Africa.

There were no positive, feel-good news stories about what a great time people had at Gwynn Oak during the festival. Instead, reports focused on the boycott and the picketing. The *Sun*'s story

Courtesy Hearst Corporation

Gwynn Oak Amusement Park during the winter off-season.

claimed that rival picketers were actually the 1962 festival's biggest attraction.

The following weekend the economic pressure continued. CIG students teamed up with CORE to picket outside Gwynn Oak while the Knights of Columbus held its annual family picnic inside the park. The *Washington Post* reported that CIG had earlier asked the Knights of Columbus, an organization with links to the Catholic Church, not to hold its yearly outing at Gwynn Oak because doing so would mean they were supporting segregation, "knowingly participating in an immoral and un-Christian act."

The picketing and CIG's dramatic statement about the picnic being "un-Christian" received an immediate response from the headquarters of the Catholic Church in Baltimore. The very next day, the superintendent of Baltimore's Catholic schools announced that parochial schools would no longer hold picnics at Gwynn Oak. He added that Archbishop Lawrence J. Shehan had reached that decision several months earlier. Now that the archbishop's boycott order was reported publicly, other organizations began boycotting Gwynn Oak, too—bad news for the park's financial future. As James Price noted, picnics and company parties were "the backbone of the amusement park business." The economic squeeze was on.

RAW EMOTION

Although the 1962 Gwynn Oak campaign didn't end Jim Crow at the park, it put Gwynn Oak's owners on the defensive. They had to justify their segregation policy to news reporters. David Price, one of the owners, explained to a *Sun* reporter that he felt the "public is not ready" for blacks to be admitted and that to do so would "destroy the business."

He was expressing a feeling that was still common among some white Baltimoreans, an unwillingness on the part of certain segments of the community to accept integration. Several episodes of racial friction cropped up in Baltimore that year. Housing was a particularly volatile topic. Back in 1948, the U.S. Supreme Court had struck down the restrictive rules that kept blacks from living in certain neighborhoods, an important victory for the NAACP's legal team. Many neighborhoods still remained segregated, but gradually some African American families began to move into previously all-white areas. Certain real estate agents exploited the situation with a practice called "blockbusting." Agents would scare white homeowners into feeling they had to sell their homes in a hurry, before blacks moved in, which might cause home prices to fall. The agents created such a sense of emergency that white homeowners sold their homes to the agents for much *less* than the houses were worth. Then the agents raised the prices and sold the homes to black families for much *more* than the agents had paid.

City officials tried to put an end to blockbusting, and community organizations worked hard to help neighborhoods deal

Black and white youngsters swim at Baltimore's Riverside Park pool, August 1962.

Courtesy Baltimore Sun

calmly with the transitions, but emotions ran high. For example, in 1962, threats made against a Native American family kept them from moving into a white Baltimore neighborhood. A black friend of that family had been helping them move. A rock was hurled through their car window, and an angry white mob of about 2,000 people gathered, shouting insults at the family.

Emotions also ran high during the summer of 1962 at a public swimming pool in Riverside Park, located in South Baltimore, a largely white area. City-owned pools had been officially integrated since the mid-1950s, but African Americans had generally stayed away from pools in white neighborhoods. The local NAACP decided it was time to change that. For several days in August 1962, Juanita Jackson Mitchell, her son Clarence, and other NAACP members accompanied small groups of black youngsters to the Riverside pool. Angry white hecklers showed up, too, shouting insults and throwing rocks. A bomb scare closed the pool during one of the black children's visits. Sometimes a few members of F.A.N., the segregationist group, joined the hecklers. Dozens of police officers patrolled the park, often with police dogs, to keep

Courtesy Hearst Corporation

Police and NAACP volunteers escort African American youngsters home from the pool at Riverside Park, September 1962. An 11-year-old who helped integrate the pool that summer was Elijah Cummings, who became a U.S. Congressman in 1996.

the situation from getting out of control. When the black youngsters left the pool, police escorted them safely out of the area and arrested some members of the white mob that harassed the young swimmers.

NO NATIONS SUCCESS SPREADS

The *No* Nations strategy also provided CORE with another victory, one that was actually more typical of the NAACP. This new victory came in a court case, which grew out of the arrests of Walter Carter and John Roemer at Gwynn Oak on August 25, 1962, the arrests that triggered the boycott that turned 1962's festival into a *No* Nations one.

Up until then, most people arrested in civil rights protests in Maryland had their cases decided by a judge—not by a jury of twelve fellow citizens. A judge would hear the evidence and decide whether protestors were guilty. This was a quicker way of handling arrests than having a long, formal jury trial. In the past, Maryland judges had always found civil rights protestors guilty, although the NAACP often appealed the convictions and some were overturned.

CORE tried a different tactic with the Carter-Roemer arrest case. Both men requested, as they had a right to do, that their guilt or innocence be decided by a jury.

Cases can turn out differently, depending on whether they're heard by just a judge or by a jury. When a judge hears a case, the judge might simply look to see whether a law was broken, and if so, find the protestors guilty. That's what had happened with the five CORE volunteers arrested at Gwynn Oak in 1959. A Baltimore County judge implied that he had no choice but to find them guilty because they had in fact broken the Trespass Law by not leaving the park. The judge explained, "Changes in the rule of law . . . are for the Legislature and not the judicial branch of the government."

A jury, on the other hand, may take other things into consideration. "A jury is more apt to decide based on emotion and facts than on the law," said New York Law School professor Carol Buckler. "There's a legal term for its use as a defense strategy: jury nullification." That means a jury can ignore or "nullify" a law (declare it has no force) if they feel the law isn't fair and just.

Thirty years earlier, a lawyer might not have chosen a jury trial for a civil rights case in Maryland because segregationist feelings were widespread and juries were all-white. By the time the Walter Carter and John Roemer case came to trial in early 1963, diehard support for segregation in Maryland had lessened somewhat. Fred E. Weisgal, the volunteer lawyer who helped CORE in this case, felt he had a good chance of persuading at least a few jury

PERSONAL PROTEST

Billie Garner Brown was one of the first blacks to graduate from a Baltimore private school. In 1962, during her senior year at the Park School, she went out to lunch with some white classmates, who drove to a White Coffee Pot, not remembering that she wouldn't be allowed inside. One girl suggested Billie pretend to be from Argentina. She tried to speak with a Spanish accent, but when the manager asked if she was from Puerto Rico, Billie answered by mistake in French, "*Oui.*" The manager didn't notice anything wrong and let her stay. After lunch, a white friend asked the manager if he ever served "Negroes." "Absolutely not," he said. She replied, "Well, you just did!" The girls raced to the car and sped off back to school.

members that using the Trespass Law against civil rights protestors was unfair. A few was all he needed, to prevent a jury from reaching a unanimous guilty decision.

During the trial, Mr. Weisgal explained to the jurors that the Trespass Law was not designed to enforce segregation. Having the police use the Trespass Law to prevent blacks from going to Gwynn Oak meant that the police—and the government—were actually supporting segregation, which some jurors might not want the government to be doing. He told them they could base their decision on "morals," explaining that, "When the law is wrong, the jury has the right to interpret the law to make it right."

To emphasize this point, he read out loud to the jurors the words that were written on an official sign posted on the courtroom wall, right under the Seal of the State of Maryland: "EQUALITY AND LIBERTY UNDER THE LAW IS THE FOUNDATION OF A GOVERNMENT OF FREE PEOPLE."

That clinched it. Jury members deliberated for a little over an hour. Six voted "guilty"—six voted "not guilty." The case was declared a mistrial and was never tried again.

EQUALITY AND LIBERTY
UNDER THE LAW
IS THE FOUNDATION
OF A GOVERNMENT
OF FREE PEOPLE

—Sign on a Baltimore County
courtroom wall,
March 1963

This March 8, 1963, court decision marked the first time civil rights protestors in Maryland avoided being convicted on trespassing charges. There was only one African American on the jury, which meant that most jurors who voted "not guilty" were white, quite an accomplishment in a Southern-leaning state. Mr. Weisgal told the *Afro-American*, "There is no doubt in my mind that the Trespass Law is on its way out. This shows that people are very upset about a law which legalizes discrimination."

The trial received a lot of publicity. News stories about white jurors voting "not guilty" might make it easier for CORE to recruit demonstrators for that summer's protests at Gwynn Oak.

During the same month as this court decision, civil rights supporters scored another legal victory when Maryland's legislature followed Baltimore's lead and passed a Maryland Public Accommodations Law. This new law, which would go into effect in June 1963, applied only to half the counties in the state, but in those counties it outlawed Jim Crow in restaurants and hotels, as Baltimore's law had done the year before. The new state law covered Baltimore County, where Gwynn Oak was located, but because the law didn't include amusement parks, Gwynn Oak was able to stick with Jim Crow.

Maryland's governor was proud that his state had become the first in the southern part of the country to pass a law ending at least some aspects of Jim Crow. State pride could prove helpful that summer at Gwynn Oak. If CORE could create a situation that challenged the state's new image by showing that Maryland was still a stronghold of discrimination, that might persuade government officials to pressure Gwynn Oak to change.

"One hundred years of delay have passed since President Lincoln freed the slaves, yet their heirs, their grandsons, are not fully free. . . . This Nation, for all its hopes and all its boasts, will not be fully free until all its citizens are free."

—President John F. Kennedy, June 11, 1963

A BOLD, NEW PLAN
1963

THE SUCCESS OF THE *No* Nations Festival, along with CORE's court victory in March 1963 and the new Maryland anti–Jim Crow law, gave members of Baltimore CORE a feeling of optimism. Also energizing was the wave of sit-ins they were staging around the state, including a blitz of them in several locations during one weekend in December 1962. Edward Chance, a new CORE volunteer who helped organize that busy weekend, told an *Afro-American* reporter, "This was only the start. We plan to demonstrate, picket and write to our legislators until every segregated door in Maryland is opened."

With the summer of 1963 approaching, CORE's leaders began to think about what kind of pressure they were going to exert on Gwynn Oak that year. One tactic led the list: mass arrests.

CORE had learned from Baltimore college students just how effective mass arrests could be, with the huge success in February that year of the student protests at the Northwood Shopping Center movie theater. (See chapter 7.) An even more dramatic use of mass arrests took place that spring in Birmingham, Alabama.

The Birmingham protests, organized by Dr. King and his Southern Christian Leadership Conference, began in April 1963 with picketing, sit-ins, and marches. The demonstrations had several goals, among them ending segregation at Birmingham's lunch counters and department stores, increasing black employment, and opening city parks to all. In the first week, about 200 people were arrested, but there wasn't much national press coverage until the second week, when Dr. King was arrested and spent a week in jail. While in jail, he wrote an inspiring letter that was smuggled out and published later as *Letter from Birmingham City Jail*. In it, he explained why he was willing to risk arrest.

Soon after his arrest, the Birmingham protest escalated. Organizers had been unable to recruit enough adults willing to be arrested, but young people were eager to help. On May 2, after receiving training in nonviolent resistance, more than a thousand Birmingham students—high schoolers and younger—walked out

A police dog attacks a young man in Birmingham, Alabama, May 1963.

of school and marched downtown. About five hundred were arrested. During the next week, Birmingham students continued marching and landing in jail. Adults joined in, too. Altogether, more than 2,400 people were arrested. Birmingham jails were so full that if the protests continued, prisoners would have to be moved to the city's sports stadium.

Most protestors stayed true to Gandhian nonviolence, even after police knocked youngsters down with blasts from fire hoses and used dogs to attack people. Dramatic photos of this brutality filled newspapers and TV screens, shocking people around the world, including President Kennedy, who stepped in to try to end the crisis. He sent a representative to Birmingham to get negotiations started. By May 10, Birmingham's white leaders agreed to many of Dr. King's demands. But a lot of white Alabamans were unhappy with the agreement and violence erupted the next day. Bombs exploded in Birmingham at the home of Dr. King's brother and at the motel where Dr. King had been staying, although he had left town by then. Some African Americans, angry about the bombings, abandoned nonviolence for a night of rioting. Dr. King returned to the city and helped restore calm in the black community. President Kennedy stationed troops near Birmingham to help prevent more violence.

FREE BY '63

The courage shown by Birmingham protestors inspired other demonstrations around the country. In May 1963, hundreds of young people were arrested during protests in Mississippi and North Carolina. In June, there were mass arrests in Georgia. Even with protests that didn't use mass arrests, there was a new intensity to demonstrations both in the South and in such non-Southern cities as Philadelphia, Los Angeles, and New York, where protestors focused on inequalities in job opportunities.

There was a feeling that the nation might achieve the goal that the NAACP had set nearly ten years earlier, when it began using the slogan "Free By '63." That reminded people that 1963 would be the 100th anniversary of the Emancipation Proclamation, a good time to finish the job the proclamation had started.

The Birmingham protests also motivated President Kennedy to give a stirring speech on TV and radio on the evening of June 11, 1963. He spoke out strongly that night against segregation and announced that he wanted Congress to pass a law that would "give all Americans the right to be served in facilities which are open to the public." A few hours later, however, a tragedy occurred in Jackson, Mississippi, showing that passing such a law wouldn't be easy because some whites were willing to take extreme measures to hold onto segregation.

Not long after the President's speech was broadcast, Medgar Evers, head of the Mississippi branch of the NAACP, was shot and killed as he returned to his home in Jackson. He was carrying an armload of T-shirts emblazoned with the words "Jim Crow Must

AP Photo/Horace Cort

May 4, 1963, Alabama Highway Patrol officers arrest Zev Aelony, one of ten CORE and SNCC members who set out from Tennessee to try to finish Bill Moore's Freedom March. Mr. Aelony had been arrested earlier in Mississippi when he was a Freedom Rider.

Go." The murder of this African American leader by a segregationist sent shockwaves through the civil rights movement.

Another murder earlier that year had also shocked many people, especially those in Baltimore's chapter of CORE. One of its white members, William (Bill) Moore, a Baltimore postal worker, had been gunned down on April 23, 1963, on an Alabama highway. He had been on a one-man Freedom March from Tennessee to Mississippi, wearing a sign that said "EQUAL RIGHTS FOR ALL (MISSISSIPPI OR BUST)." His goal was to deliver a letter on civil rights to Mississippi's governor. About a week after his murder, two small groups tried to complete his journey. These eighteen "Freedom Walkers"—college students and members of CORE, SNCC, and other groups—failed to complete the mission because they were arrested in Alabama. In mid-June and also in early August, hundreds of people were arrested in Gadsden, Alabama, for trying once again to resume Bill Moore's walk. They too never made it to Mississippi to deliver his letter.

These murders and arrests showed that white opposition to integration was still fierce in the Deep South. Strong pressure would need to be brought on members of Congress to encourage enough of them to do the right thing and vote for anti–Jim Crow laws. Dr. King hoped to apply such pressure with the huge March on Washington that he was organizing for August 28, 1963.

During the summer of 1963, members of Baltimore CORE helped make arrangements for this upcoming March on Washington, while also holding sit-ins in western Maryland. But their main focus that summer was Gwynn Oak.

James Farmer, CORE's national director, had said that people needed to create a crisis in order to bring about change. That's exactly what Baltimore CORE hoped to do at Gwynn Oak. Mass arrests seemed the best way to get the job done.

A LUCKY BREAK

CORE picked a special day for its main 1963 Gwynn Oak protest, a day that was sure to draw a lot of attention: the Fourth of July.

Highlighting the unfairness of Jim Crow on the day America celebrates its independence would deliver a powerful message.

The choice of the Fourth would also alert the press that this year's event would be different, not just another day of All Nations Day Festival picketing. "To the local press, sometimes demonstrations get to be old hat," said John Roemer. "We had to keep coming up with new 'angles' to keep the press interested, to keep the news fresh." The Fourth of July would provide such an angle. So would mass arrests.

Organizing a successful mass arrest protest required a lot of planning—and a bit of luck. CORE had contacts with many student groups and activist organizations, both in Baltimore and elsewhere. That helped in rounding up enough protestors to make an impact. Walter Carter even did some recruiting that spring in a western Maryland jail cell. He was arrested during a sit-in there and shared a cell with Walter South, a New York CORE member who had brought two busloads of New Yorkers for the sit-in. When Mr. South heard what was being planned in July for Gwynn Oak, he promised to once again bring busloads of New Yorkers to Maryland. John Roemer had done some pre-planning, too. The year before, he had met two New York City union leaders at a Gwynn Oak protest. "They saw what we were going through down here," he explained. "They went back to New York, talked it up, and helped galvanize people for 1963."

But just having a large crowd might not be enough to win the kind of national news coverage that made a difference in Birmingham. To entice more reporters to cover the event, it would help if there were something out-of-the ordinary about the protestors.

This is where luck came in. A special category of individuals had just decided in June 1963 to put their bodies on the line—the picket line—and begin protesting Jim Crow. These new protestors were religious leaders.

Of course, many African American ministers had taken part in civil rights protests, but not many white clergy had. On June 7, 1963, the National Council of Churches decided at its annual meeting in New York City that instead of just preaching about

ON-THE-SPOT LEARNING

It wasn't only Baltimore CORE that was figuring out along the way how to run a protest. So was Dr. King. He and his associates debated long and hard about what to do in Birmingham in 1963 because the year before things hadn't gone well for them in Albany, Georgia. "What we learned from our mistakes in Albany helped our later campaigns in other cities to be more effective," wrote Dr. King. He felt the goals in Albany had been too broad. Another problem: not much press coverage. That's because Albany's police chief, Laurie Pritchett, had studied up on Gandhi and Dr. King to figure out how to blunt the impact of the protest. Mr. Pritchett realized that if police didn't mistreat protestors, there would be no dramatic news reports to spark a call for change. He was right. But when "Bull" Connor, Birmingham's police chief, turned fire hoses on demonstrators in 1963, that guaranteed public outrage. President Kennedy is said to have remarked, "The civil rights movement should thank God for Bull Connor. He's helped it as much as Abraham Lincoln."

how bad Jim Crow was, ministers needed to actually *do* something to end it by taking part in "demonstrations and direct action." The council, made up of most of the country's Protestant churches, set up an Emergency Commission on Race and Religion to explore ways to help. That same month, a national group of Jewish leaders, the Central Conference of American Rabbis, met in Philadelphia and reached a similar decision, pledging that it was time for Jewish congregations to make an "all-out effort" to support civil rights.

These religious leaders were fired up and ready to protest. How lucky that the National Council of Churches learned from CORE that an opportunity was coming up in less than a month at Gwynn Oak. Several well-known Protestant pastors from around the country promised to come to Baltimore on the Fourth of July and risk being arrested. So did many of Baltimore's own religious leaders—Protestant, Catholic, and Jewish.

If large numbers of ministers, priests, and rabbis showed up on the Fourth of July, the Gwynn Oak showdown would be the first time so many religious leaders—especially white religious leaders—would be taking part in a civil rights protest. That by itself would attract press coverage. Reporters would become even more interested if a lot of religious leaders wound up being arrested.

CORE made sure national reporters knew about the Fourth of July protest. "We sent out press releases to the *New York Times* and other papers. Press coverage was absolutely important," said Alison Turaj Brown. This 25-year-old former Baltimorean had been living in New York, where she was active in CORE. The year before, she had traveled back to Maryland to take part in sit-ins in Cambridge and had been arrested. During the summer of 1963, she was in Washington helping another group, the Northern Student Movement, set up tutoring programs for minority students. When planning for the Fourth of July began to heat up, she headed back to New York to help organize things on that end.

"We were not professional press release writers, but we had all gone to college and just kind of put it together," she said. "Nobody was paid or anything. We took odd jobs to support ourselves. There was a network of people in New York who belonged to CORE, the NAACP, and Christian and Jewish organizations. We sent out releases to them. Walter South organized the clergy." He was the New York CORE member who had started planning this demonstration with Walter Carter a few months earlier in a western Maryland jail.

NEW CHAIRMAN IN CHARGE

As planning began heating up for the Fourth of July showdown at Gwynn Oak, Baltimore CORE had a new chairman. In early June, Walter Carter's term as chairman of Baltimore CORE ended. Everyone thought he would be elected again, but he decided not to run (although he continued as a member of CORE and helped with that summer's events). He was worn out emotionally and financially. His two years as chairman had involved nonstop, unpaid

This demonstration at Baltimore's main post office honored postal worker and CORE member William (Bill) Moore shortly after he was killed in Alabama on April 23, 1963, during his one-man Freedom March.

Courtesy Hearst Corporation

work organizing sit-ins and being arrested. He was also holding down a job as a social worker to support his family. On May 30, he had been arrested again with seven other CORE picketers at an earlier-than-usual Gwynn Oak demonstration. This protest and another in mid-May had been organized to honor the memory of Bill Moore, the CORE member who was murdered a few weeks before in Alabama during his one-man Freedom March.

John Roemer reached the same decision as Walter Carter and let someone else take over as vice-chairman. "I'd been arrested a lot," he explained. "I told my wife, 'I won't do it anymore.' We had two kids, didn't have any money." As Walter Carter explained to a *Sun* reporter, "Nonviolent demonstration has been very successful. But it is also expensive."

Fortunately, Ed Chance was ready to take over as chairman. He had grown up in North Carolina. In 1963, he was working as a social worker in Baltimore, having earned his master's degree at Howard University. Ed Chance's father, William Chance, a high school principal in North Carolina, had set an example for his son by taking a stand against Jim Crow back in 1948. The elder Mr. Chance was arrested that year for not moving to the Jim Crow car on a train. NAACP lawyers appealed his arrest. In 1951, a U.S. Court of Appeals overturned his conviction. It's not surprising that his 30-year-old son, Ed, would want to follow his father's lead and find a way to carry on the struggle to end segregation.

Ed Chance had already shown his organizational ability in coordinating CORE's statewide blitz of sit-ins in December 1962. More recently, in early May he helped set up a memorial service for Bill Moore that was attended by hundreds of mourners at a Unitarian church in downtown Baltimore. These two leaders—Ed Chance and Walter Carter—had both grown up in the South and had come to Baltimore to work as social workers, expecting better conditions. Perhaps that's why they spent so much time volunteering with CORE, to make reality live up to their expectations.

GETTING READY

CORE had already held a few small demonstrations that spring at Gwynn Oak, one on May 18 at which nineteen protestors were arrested, and the one on May 30 that led to the arrest of Walter Carter and seven others. On June 1 there was another small dem-

onstration. A Baltimore County activist had suggested that maybe CORE should cool it for a while, so as not to make county legislators unwilling to set up a new Human Relations Commission. But members of Baltimore CORE were in no mood to slow down.

Ed Chance (left), chairman of Baltimore CORE in 1963, with Rev. Frank Williams, pastor of Metropolitan Methodist Church where the pre-demonstration rally would be held on July 4, 1963.

Courtesy Baltimore Sun

In late June, CORE announced in an article in the *Afro-American* that plans were well underway for a big demonstration at Gwynn Oak on the Fourth of July. As Walter Carter explained to the *Afro* reporter, the park's owners "leave us with no other choice but to demonstrate. They have flatly refused to cooperate with us in our attempt to settle this problem without demonstrations. We have written them letters . . . but they have refused to even talk with us."

With Ed Chance in command and Charles Mason serving as chairman of CORE's organization committee, a dedicated team of volunteers was hard at work making final preparations for the history-making protests of 1963. There was lots to do:

* *Nonviolent workshop.* To make sure the protest would be nonviolent, on the morning of the Fourth of July, all demonstrators—those from Baltimore and those arriving by bus from other cities—would go first to a church in West Baltimore to receive training in good demonstration techniques. "We always did that before demonstrations to make sure that people would try as best they could to be nonviolent," said Charles Mason. Alison Turaj Brown, who helped run those workshops, explained, "The basic nonviolent training was: If you were hit, you did not hit back. If you were spit on or called names, you were to consider the source" and not talk back. "Just pray and sing loud." She showed people how to protect themselves and cover their faces in case they were attacked. The basic advice: "If in your heart you had the feeling that you would strike back, then don't come."

* *Press contacts.* National CORE notified New York reporters. Baltimore CORE made arrangements with local TV stations and newspapers to cover both the pre-demonstration gathering at the church and the demonstration. They also managed to have articles appear in the *Afro-American* the week before the demonstration giving details about where and when protestors would assemble. In an article in the July 2 *Afro*, a CORE representative explained, "We have had several

demonstrations already this year but the July 4 action really kicks off the Gwynn Oak campaign," one that he promised would include some "surprise tactics."

- *Fliers.* "We flooded the city with fliers about the demonstration," said Charles Mason. "I personally would load up my car—a little white two-seater MGA—with fliers and go from East Baltimore to West Baltimore and to all the churches and restaurants, any place that people would go."

- *Signing up recruits.* "I worked for CORE as a secretary in the office," said Marie Williams, who was 20 years old in 1963. "I didn't get paid. I was a volunteer. Mostly there wasn't anybody in the office but me. I signed people up to be demonstrators. People would come in and want to demonstrate, and I would put their name on the list." She had started volunteering during high school, at the suggestion of her sister, Carolyn Stith, "who was always involved in politics" and had been arrested that May with Walter Carter at the earlier Gwynn Oak protest.

- *Co-Sponsors.* CORE reached out to local and national groups to serve as co-sponsors of the demonstration. All co-sponsors urged their members to participate, and some arranged for buses to bring out-of-town demonstrators. The Roman Catholic Archdiocese of Baltimore, one of the co-sponsors, assigned Rev. Austin J. Healy as Archbishop Shehan's official representative at the protest. Other local co-sponsors included Baltimore's Interfaith Committee on Human Rights (made up of Protestant, Catholic, and Jewish clergy), the Interdenominational Ministerial Alliance, and the Maryland Council of Churches. Having so many religious organizations as co-sponsors could help boost the courage of local clergy who might be concerned that some members of their congregations would oppose the idea of religious leaders taking part in demonstrations, as indeed turned out to be the case. Additional co-sponsors included CIG, Campus Americans for Democratic Action, a New York labor union, and other student and peace groups. The *New York Times* estimated that forty groups took part.

- *Police plans.* Ed Chance, Walter Carter, and Eugene King, a Baltimore County activist, met with Baltimore County's new police chief, Robert Lally, to make plans for the hundreds of people that organizers predicted would be arrested. Police brutality in other cities had brought press attention, but Ed Chance did not want to put protestors' safety at risk. He had enough of a headline grabber with religious leaders participating. Chief Lally, formerly the assistant chief of the FBI office in Baltimore, figured out how to handle the arrests peacefully so his officers wouldn't be featured on the evening news for brutalizing protestors. He also worked out ways to protect demonstrators from angry whites. Ed Chance described this meeting with Chief Lally in an article in the July 2 issue of the *Afro-American* in which he said, "Chief Lally promised to arrest anyone who starts any violence, including white customers at the park." This might help calm the fears of those who weren't sure about joining the protest, an understandable concern given recent violence not only in Birmingham and on that Alabama highway where Bill Moore was killed, but also in Cambridge, Maryland. White mobs in that Eastern Shore city had responded violently to recent sit-ins there, prompting Maryland's governor to call in National Guard troops.

As the day of the demonstration neared, CORE members had a feeling of optimism about the Fourth of July showdown. "The time had come," said Rev. Marion C. Bascom, reflecting the feeling of many Baltimore activists. "There was a sense that the tide was turning," noted Mike Furstenberg, a college freshman in 1963 who was ready to walk a picket line and cool his heels in a county jail if that's what it took to end Jim Crow at Gwynn Oak.

". . . any individual who breaks a law that conscience tells him is unjust, and willingly accepts the penalty by staying in jail to arouse the conscience of the community over its injustice, is in reality expressing the very highest respect for law."

—Rev. Dr. Martin Luther King, Jr.,
Letter from Birmingham City Jail, 1963

© James Singewald

FOURTH OF JULY
SHOWDOWN
1963

"THE CHURCHES IN THIS COUNTRY have for a long time been saying a great deal about discrimination," said Rev. Dr. Eugene Carson Blake, a white Presbyterian minister speaking to the huge crowd gathered at the pre-demonstration rally on Thursday morning, July 4, 1963. "Almost all the churches have made the right statements, but we can no longer let the burden of winning freedom for the Negro or any other oppressed people be the burden of the oppressed people themselves." With those rousing words, Dr. Blake, national head of the United Presbyterian Church, set the tone for the day's Operation Gwynn Oak.

More than 300 people showed up that morning for the rally at Metropolitan Methodist Church in an African American neighborhood in West Baltimore. Four buses had brought about 200 demonstrators from New York City. Another busload of protestors rolled in from Philadelphia. Others came from Washington, D.C., and as far away as New Haven, Connecticut, to join Baltimoreans in taking a firm stand against Jim Crow at Gwynn Oak Amusement Park.

To the delight of Baltimore CORE members, more than two dozen clergymen were there, some from Baltimore, as well as several prominent national religious leaders. Dr. Blake, who came from New York City to join the protest, was the most famous of the out-of-towners and was responsible for many of the other clergy being there. He had introduced the resolution at the June meeting of the National Council of Churches that persuaded council members to begin taking part in civil rights demonstrations.

A local TV station recorded the meeting at the church. Also on the scene were reporters from Baltimore newspapers, as well as some from out-of-town papers such as the *New York Times* and *Washington Post*.

So far, all was going as planned. Simply having famous pastors there would make this demonstration different from earlier Gwynn Oak protests. In addition, most of the faces in the crowd were white, another new development for civil rights protests. A big white turnout would lead to more news stories and undercut the claim by Gwynn Oak's owners that whites and blacks were "not ready" to do things together.

Among the white participants were Lois B. Feinblatt and other members of the civil rights committee at her temple, Baltimore Hebrew Congregation. "Our rabbi, Morris Lieberman, was very active in civil rights, and he encouraged members of the congregation to go," said Ms. Feinblatt. "He was a fabulous religious leader who inspired people to get out there and do something, to put Jewish principles into action." Members of three other local Jewish congregations were also there with their rabbis.

After arriving at the church, protestors went to the basement for a workshop on protest techniques. Leo Burroughs, Jr., a 21-year-old CORE volunteer, worked with Dr. Blake to show how to fend off an attack. Then demonstrators crowded into the sanctuary where they got in the mood for the day's events by singing the unofficial anthem of the civil rights movement, "We Shall Overcome."

Next, several religious leaders spoke to the crowd. Dr. Blake explained that he had come to support black preachers who had "been carrying the burden of active demonstrations."

Baltimore's Rev. Marion C. Bascom also spoke from the pulpit that day. Earlier in the year, this African American minister had urged CIG college students to risk arrest during their movie theater protest. At that time he wasn't ready to be arrested himself. Now he was, as he explained to the cheering Fourth of July protestors: "I am the one who said all along I will not go to jail, but I will help others who go. But this morning I said to myself I have nothing to lose but my chains. So if I do not preach at my pulpit Sunday morning, it might be the most eloquent sermon I ever preached."

THE ARRESTS BEGIN

In early afternoon, demonstrators left the church and piled into buses and cars to head over to Gwynn Oak. They arrived just before 3:00 P.M. It was a hot, sunny day. Tension had been building at the park for hours. Everyone at Gwynn Oak knew demonstrators were coming but had thought the protest would start earlier. It would have, if buses from out of town hadn't arrived later than expected.

About fifty Baltimore County police officers were waiting for the protestors, along with twenty-five private security guards hired by the park. Inside the park, about 1,500 customers—all white—were having fun on the merry-go-round and other rides.

In addition, swarms of news reporters and photographers were there, ready to cover the event. Some interviewed James Price, one of the park's owners, as he stood guard at the front entrance. He gave reporters his usual reason for sticking with Jim Crow: "We live in an area where the white man does not accept the Negro on a social basis. It's a matter of economic survival." He stated firmly, "We are not going to let them in."

As protestors arrived, some began picketing, walking in a line, back and forth along the median strip of the avenue in front of the park's entrance, singing protest songs and carrying signs with such slogans as "SEGREGATION IS UN-AMERICAN," "EQUALITY NOW," "FREE BY '63," and "GIVE ME JUSTICE OR GIVE ME JAIL." About a dozen Catholic priests were handing out copies of a letter on "Racial Justice" from Baltimore's Archbishop Lawrence J. Shehan.

CORE had an orderly plan for the arrests. Demonstrators who didn't want to go to jail could spend the afternoon on the picket line. Those who chose arrest were divided into small groups of about ten people, making sure that each contingent contained both blacks and whites. One at a time, the groups would try to enter the park.

The first group to walk up to the ticket booth included the day's most newsworthy demonstrators: Dr. Blake and Bishop Daniel Corrigan, an important national leader of the Episcopal Church. Also in the first group were Rev. Bascom, CORE's Ed Chance, the Urban League's Furman Templeton, and Father Joseph Connolly, a Catholic priest who was one of the three co-chairmen of Baltimore's Interfaith Committee. The Jewish and Protestant co-chairmen of that committee—Rabbi Morris Lieberman and Rev. John Middaugh—were arrested with later groups.

As each group reached the ticket booth, one of the park's owners stopped them. He or an assistant read aloud the Maryland Trespass Law. When demonstrators refused to leave, police officers led them out to police vans or school buses, which took them to a nearby police station.

Courtesy Baltimore Sun

Rev. Dr. Eugene Carson Blake (second from left), Father Joseph M. Connolly (far left) and Rev. Marion C. Bascom (fourth from left) after being arrested at Gwynn Oak on July 4, 1963.

Catholic, Protestant, and Jewish clergymen, arrested at Gwynn Oak on July 4, 1963, on the bus that took them to the police station.

AP Photo/William A. Smith

Photographers snapped history-making photos of solemn religious leaders being arrested. Those images would appear in the next day's newspapers. Dr. Blake told reporters, "I don't know if the Trespass Law of the State of Maryland is constitutional but I am sure it is not right if it allows property rights to be a constant public affront to the Negro community."

For the next three hours, group after group approached the ticket booth and then walked out under arrest, accompanied by police officers, to board police vans and buses. Some protestors sat on the ground by the ticket booth, refused to budge when arrested, and had to be carried out by the police. After arriving at the police station, some protestors refused to get off the bus and had to be carried into the station. Police generally treated demonstrators well, but a few officers grumbled about having to carry protestors on such a hot afternoon.

On the trip to jail, protestors sang "We Shall Overcome" and also—in honor of the Fourth of July—"The Star-Spangled Banner." Many kept singing as they marched into the police station and waited to be booked.

When a reporter asked Rabbi Lieberman why he had joined other clergy to be arrested, he smiled and said, "I think every American should celebrate the Fourth of July."

TENSE MOMENTS

A different kind of crowd of several hundred people gathered near the park's entrance—a mob of angry whites who wanted Gwynn Oak to remain a whites-only park. They shouted insults and curses at the demonstrators and cheered when demonstrators were led to police vans. So did white customers inside the park, who stopped going on rides to watch the protest. A boisterous pack of teenagers showed up waving Confederate flags. They ripped up copies of Archbishop Shehan's letter on "Racial Justice." Police chased them away.

When the insult-shouting crowd at the front gate grew too rowdy, the police roped off the area to keep them away from demonstrators. One officer told the mob that they could be arrested along with the protestors. Chief Lally warned his own officers and the park's guards that they could be arrested as well if they used more force than was necessary.

"We had excellent cooperation from the police," said Eugene King, a local activist who spent much of the afternoon riding around with the police chief, helping keep things under control. At the police station, several clergymen thanked the police for making sure the afternoon stayed nonviolent.

Although there wasn't any major violence, there were some tense moments. One occurred before the demonstration started. State Senator Verda Welcome arrived at the park before the other demonstrators to see if she could negotiate a settlement. "I was friendly with one of the owners of the park, and I thought maybe I could talk him into letting the people come in," said Senator Welcome, who had recently been elected to the Maryland State Senate.

When she drove into the Gwynn Oak parking lot, a crowd of angry white men surrounded her car, yelling, "You can't come in

State Senator Verda Welcome with a Baltimore County Police officer at Gwynn Oak, July 4, 1963.

Courtesy Afro-American Newspapers Archives

here!" They prevented her from leaving her car. She shouted for help to a police officer she saw in the distance. When the men saw the officer, they left. If that officer hadn't shown up, she realized that the gang of men "could've done practically anything. . . . These guys had daggers in their eyes." She spoke with one of the park's owners, who said he was "so embarrassed" that the men had threatened her. But he wouldn't agree to her request that the park open to blacks. "He was willing, but his brother wasn't," she said.

A different disturbance occurred when the demonstration was first getting underway. Someone threw a rock that hit CORE's Charles Mason in the head, briefly knocking him unconscious. "I was getting the picket line in order, and the hecklers weren't that far from us," he said. "I wasn't really surprised. I expected that would happen sooner or later. Before, at other events, I was pushed and shoved, but nothing that physical. I had to leave the demonstration to get stitches." The rock-thrower was never caught.

Another dangerous situation arose when a group of demonstrators decided not to follow CORE's group-by-group arrest plan. Instead, they tried to enter Gwynn Oak by going around to the back of the park, where they first had to wade across a small stream to enter the park grounds. As they headed into the park, two policemen stopped them and asked them to wait there until a park official could come read them the Trespass Law. As they waited, a hostile crowd surrounded them. Someone in the crowd threw a cherry bomb which cut the leg of one of the protestors, a 26-year-old secretary from New York. Police gave her first aid and led the others to a school bus so they could be arrested before the situation spiraled out of control.

Courtesy Afro-American Newspapers Archives

That evening, outside the police station where many of the arrested had been taken, a small group of civil rights supporters picketed. One young CIG member carried a sign that said, "THE WORLD IS WATCHING—LET'S PUT AN END TO RACIAL DISCRIMINATION." Some hecklers

Some protestors arrested at Gwynn Oak refused to walk to police buses and had to be carried.

showed up to harass these picketers. One heckler was arrested. Two other white men were arrested for throwing firecrackers at picketers from a passing car. They also apparently threw a firecracker that slightly injured two 21-year-old protestors, Danny Schechter and Marlene Stevens, who had gone to a nearby diner to get something to eat. The diner refused to serve them, and as they walked away, the firecracker was hurled at these two young people, who were working in Baltimore that summer, helping the Northern Student Movement set up a tutoring center for kids.

STUDENT SUPPORT

Although the ministers, priests, and rabbis were the headline-grabbers, most of the day's demonstrators were young people—college students, recent college graduates, and a few high schoolers. Some were Baltimoreans, including Senator Welcome's daughter, Mary Sue, who was then a 19-year-old Morgan student, and Leo Burroughs, Jr., a recent Morgan graduate. Michael Mitchell was there, too. At age 17, he had just graduated from high school. He had two roles that day: to walk the picket line, as he had been doing for years at civil rights protests, and to serve as the official

Gwynn Oak protestors used lipstick to write CORE's slogan—"Freedom Now"—on the side of the bus that took them to the police station.

Courtesy Hearst Corporation

driver for his mother, Juanita Jackson Mitchell, who was there to provide legal help for the demonstrators.

Mike Furstenberg, an 18-year-old who was home after his freshman year at the University of Chicago, had taken part in some earlier protests but had never been arrested before. "It was a big step, being arrested, something I wanted to do," he said. "My father made a little fun of me about being arrested, that it was a badge of honor. But it really was. It meant something. It was a matter of faith, that there was a higher law that transcended what was the law of the land at that time." He had planned to go to the protest with two friends from high school. "At the last minute their parents were afraid, didn't want them to do it, and they didn't. I wasn't really expecting any violence, but maybe I just didn't know any better."

Marie Williams, a 20-year-old who had been volunteering in the Baltimore CORE office, was one of the hundred or so protestors who spent the day walking the picket line. That had its own risks, "with people spitting at you, carrying on. I controlled my temper," she said. "When you see people being abused but not getting violent, that says a lot. It's more effective. If you're violent, you're just as bad as the other person." Walking that picket line and helping to support her sister, Carolyn Stith, who was arrested that day, made her feel "I was part of the movement."

Many of the college-age protestors were out-of-towners who had come on buses from New York and Philadelphia. They had been recruited by volunteers such as Jack Newfield, a 25-year-old aspiring writer who lived in New York and spent June rounding up students to fill the buses. He wrote later that he was startled by the intensity of the angry white mob at Gwynn Oak, something he wasn't used to as a white New Yorker.

One 23-year-old hadn't planned to join the protest until he made an on-the-spot decision. "My father was on the Baltimore Equal Opportunity Commission and went out to Gwynn Oak on July Fourth to keep an eye on things," said Lew Buckler, who went along on that inspection tour. He was so inspired by the protestors that "I felt it was time to take a stand. So I joined them and

Jack Newfield went on to become a prize-winning journalist. He wrote in his memoir, *Somebody's Gotta Tell It*, that while in a Baltimore jail cell after being arrested at the Fourth of July protest, he remembered another Fourth of July—the one in 1948—when he saw his first baseball game and watched Jackie Robinson steal home. Mr. Newfield said he sang "The Star-Spangled Banner" at that baseball game and in the police van that took him to jail in Baltimore, feeling proud to be an American both days.

was arrested. This was my first demonstration that involved going to jail." He had gone to high school at Poly, the special science and math school that had integrated two years before the rest of Baltimore's schools. "I was in the second class at Poly that was integrated. There was a strong feeling at the school that everything should be integrated. I think some people were fearful of integration, feeling segregation is the way things always were. But people have to look at their values and stand up for what's right instead of always being afraid."

THE ARREST TALLY

By 6:00 P.M. when the protest ended, 283 protestors had been arrested, including more than twenty religious leaders. That was a larger number of clergy than had been arrested before at any one civil rights demonstration. Eight of the pastors were from New York. The chaplain of Yale University, Rev. William Sloan Coffin, had come all the way from Connecticut with his wife, who spent the night in jail, too. Rev. Coffin had been arrested a few years earlier on a Freedom Ride down South. The other clergy were from Baltimore. Some picketed but chose not to be arrested. One minister apologized for not going to jail, explaining that he had to perform a wedding. Altogether, more than 350 people took part in the demonstration.

Of course, 283 arrests were many fewer than had been arrested earlier that year in Birmingham, Alabama. But 283 arrests were enough to overwhelm Baltimore County's police and judicial systems. Midway through the demonstration, police had to take protestors to a second police station because the one nearest the park couldn't handle any more prisoners. Fingerprinting and filling out forms for everyone took hours. Some people weren't booked until after midnight. Many requested jury trials, which would cause an ongoing crisis for the county. Robert Watts and Juanita Jackson Mitchell, NAACP volunteer lawyers, handled the legal work, helping protestors file not-guilty pleas and request jury trials.

Demonstrators had been warned to bring money to pay bail so they could go home. Many did, but others chose the jail-no-bail approach. They wanted to show that they believed strongly enough in ending discrimination that they would stay in jail. More than 150 spent the night in jail. They weren't released until after a court hearing the next evening, at which the judge let most of them go home without paying bail, if they promised to return for their trials.

Protestors who spent the night locked up were scattered in various buildings around the county because Baltimore County didn't have enough space in any one jail to hold them all. Women arrestees spent the night in a fire station, where cots were set up for them.

Mike Furstenberg recalled that his night in jail "stands out for me more than anything else. I happened to be placed in the same cell with Rev. William Sloan Coffin, the chaplain at Yale. He was a fascinating, interesting guy who carried on a kind of seminar for the twenty or thirty people who were in the cell with him. He talked about civil rights, faith, politics, what was going on around the world. It was like being in a classroom. We all slept sprawled out on the floor. It wasn't too comfortable, but it was a great learning experience."

Robert Watts said the NAACP paid him a token amount, just $100, for all he did in 1963 providing legal help at no charge to the protestors. "I was so wrapped up in this thing that I went out and represented people for nothing . . . the whole year I made $100 on civil rights cases and I was in the station house practically every morning at 8:00 and sometimes I wouldn't get back to my office until noon," he recalled. He didn't expect to be paid. He and other NAACP lawyers, including Juanita Jackson Mitchell, were glad to help protestors. He had been a judge in the late 1950s, but was back in private practice during 1963 so he could help at Gwynn Oak. Later that year, he became a judge again and served on various courts for more than twenty years.

MORE TO COME

"Dr. Blake Among 283 Held In Racial Rally in Maryland." That was the headline on a front-page story the next day in the *New York Times*. Accompanying the story was a photo of Dr. Blake stepping into a police van. The *Sun*'s story filled a page and a half of the paper. *Afro-American* coverage spread over three pages. Big news stories appeared in other Baltimore, New York, and Washington papers, in *Time* magazine, and on TV and radio.

The news reports stressed the historic nature of the demonstration. The *New York Times* described it as "the first time that so large a group of important clergymen of all three major faiths had participated together in a direct concerted protest against discrimination." News stories also pointed out that the great majority of the civil rights protestors were white.

As impressive as this Fourth of July showdown was, it didn't put an immediate end to Jim Crow at Gwynn Oak. The park's owners refused to drop their whites-only policy. That didn't discourage the protest leaders. They were ready to hold more demonstrations.

Courtesy Afro-American Newspapers Archives

State Senator Verda Welcome (far right) on the picket line at Gwynn Oak, July 4, 1963.

At the police station, while waiting to be booked, seven ministers created a committee to sponsor more protests—the Ad Hoc Committee to Desegregate Gwynn Oak Park. Ed Chance was on this committee, too. He and the seven ministers had all decided on jail-no-bail and spent the night in jail.

Setting up this new Ad Hoc Committee was a smart way to broaden the base of support for future protests. No longer would a Gwynn Oak protest be seen as something that only a few CORE activists did. It would have the stamp of approval of religious leaders. Among the African American clergy from Baltimore who created this new committee were Rev. Bascom, Rev. Vernon Dobson, and Rev. Frank Williams, whose church had hosted the morning rally. Two white ministers were also founding members of the committee—an Episcopal minister from New York and Rev. Chester Wickwire, the chaplain at Johns Hopkins University.

Committee members contacted Walter Carter (who had chosen not to be arrested) so that he could tell reporters when the next demonstration would take place: Sunday afternoon July 7, three days away. They had learned from the Northwood Theatre and Birmingham protests the value of keeping up the pressure.

The county judicial system was strained to the limit. More arrests on Sunday would make matters worse. That prompted Baltimore County's chief executive, Spiro T. Agnew, to try to discourage activists from holding more protests. The *Washington Post* reported that he promised to support a law that would force the park to integrate if a new Baltimore County Human Relations Commission—which he hoped would be set up on Monday—failed to persuade the park's owners to drop segregation.

CORE and the new Ad-Hoc Committee weren't going to wait for any soon-to-be-established commission. Mass arrests—and massive publicity—had created a crisis at Gwynn Oak on the Fourth. They hoped it would create even more of a crisis on Sunday.

Most of the out-of-town protestors would be gone by Sunday. There wouldn't be time to round up more. This time, Baltimoreans would have to step up and come out in force.

The *Sun* and the *Afro-American* helped by printing stories that told where and when demonstrators should meet for Sunday's protest. The papers reported that local clergy would talk up the demonstration during services. The *Sun* noted also that a boycott of Gwynn Oak was being considered for later.

Of course, all this news coverage let segregationists know about Sunday's event, too. They could be expected to come out in force as well, all fired up to defend one of the last outposts of Jim Crow in the Baltimore area. The stage was set for a potentially violent face-off on Sunday, with plenty of TV and newspaper reporters on hand to record what would happen.

"It's important to stick up for and protect the rights of everybody."

—Lydia Phinney Wilkins, from a July 2009 interview

© James Singewald

FACING A
HOSTILE CROWD
1963

O N SUNDAY, JULY 7, Baltimoreans did indeed turn out in large numbers for that day's demonstration at Gwynn Oak Amusement Park—both those opposed to Jim Crow and those definitely in favor of it. The 300 civil rights protestors were outnumbered by a mob of more than 1,500 segregationists who were more rowdy, more hostile, and much more willing to hurl rocks than the hecklers on the Fourth of July had been. Sunday's angry mob included about a dozen members of the local white-power segregationist group F.A.N. (Fighting American Nationalists), who carried signs that said "KEEP GWYNN OAK WHITE," "INTEGRATION STINKS," and "U.S. FOR WHITES—AFRICA FOR BLACKS."

The civil rights protestors managed for the most part to stick to their plan of orderly arrests and won the moral high ground with their nonviolent behavior, but it wasn't easy. At one point, a few civil rights protestors forgot their nonviolence training and shouted insults back at the hecklers. Protest organizers asked those stressed-out demonstrators to leave the picket line. It was to be a long, hot afternoon.

The day had begun as it had on the Fourth of July—with a non-violence workshop and rally for civil rights protestors at Metropolitan Methodist Church. Plenty of local rabbis, ministers, and priests joined the Sunday protest, but there were no high-profile, national religious leaders as there had been three days earlier. However, several of those national clergy, including Rev. Dr. Eugene Carson Blake, would be back in Baltimore the next day for a court hearing in connection with their arrests at the earlier demonstration.

Baltimore's Father Joseph Connolly brought sixty members of his congregation to Sunday's event. About a hundred members of three other local Catholic parishes were there. Altogether, nearly half the day's protestors came from Catholic churches. Many were members of largely African American parishes, but there was also white Catholic participation. Father Connolly noted that this kind of parish involvement was a history-making first for Catholicism in Maryland, the first time "parishes as parishes are participating in a civil rights demonstration."

Rev. Marion C. Bascom spoke to the protestors gathered at the church, energizing them this time by adapting the words of a familiar spiritual: "Go down to Gwynn Oak and tell the Prices to let our people go."

Some protestors were repeaters, having already been arrested on July 4. Lew Buckler was glad to be back because, as he noted proudly, "This time it wasn't just clergy and a bunch of kids from New York. The second demonstration showed strong Baltimore support."

Some out-of-towners were there as well. Two of them persuaded Baltimorean Arthur Waskow to join the protest. Mr. Waskow, age 30, had grown up in Baltimore but was living in Washington, D.C., that summer, working at the Peace Research Institute while also finishing up writing his PhD thesis for a graduate program he was in at the University of Wisconsin-Madison. On July 4, he received a phone call from Carol McEldowney, a young co-worker of his. She and a friend, Harvard student Todd Gitlin, had just been arrested at Gwynn Oak. They were members of a new student group—Students for a Democratic Society (SDS)—that helped recruit young people for the demonstration. She phoned Arthur

Waskow to ask if he could find a way to send money to Baltimore to pay their bail so they could get out of jail.

He arranged to send the bail money, but then felt terrible about not having been at the demonstration himself. He thought he should have been there, to try to change the park where he had gone on rides as a kid and where his high school class held its senior prom. Instead, he had been reading a copy of the Declaration of Independence, a document he liked to read every Fourth of July. "I realized how absurd it was to celebrate a revolution for liberty by reading about it, instead of joining it," he wrote later. When he heard that there would be another demonstration, he arranged to meet his SDS friends at Sunday's pre-demonstration rally at the Baltimore church. He had to drive up to Baltimore that day anyway, to bring the last chapter of his PhD thesis to his mother so she could type it up for him. It was about race riots. He hoped there wouldn't be one at Gwynn Oak.

THREE BOYS IN A POLICE CAR

Three young white boys—Tom Coleman, age eight, his six-year-old brother, John, and their baby brother, Steve, just five months old—were at Sunday's demonstration, too. Photos of them at the protest appeared in newspapers the next day and played a part in opening up Gwynn Oak's merry-go-round.

The Coleman family lived in a small, largely white town near Baltimore. Tom and John didn't know any black kids—there weren't any at their elementary school. But their parents had explained to them about the unfairness of Jim Crow. Their father, James Coleman, was a sociology professor at Johns Hopkins University. A few years later, he wrote an important study—the Coleman Report—on equality of educational opportunity in American schools. The boys' mother, Lucille Coleman, was a member of Baltimore CORE and had participated in some earlier demonstrations, although not at Gwynn Oak. "We knew all about segregation," explained Tom Coleman. "There was a lunch-counter sit-in in our town. We knew segregation wasn't right."

Lu Coleman had been moved by news reports of the demonstrations in Birmingham, Alabama, where people let their children take part in protests. News stories about the Fourth of July protest at Gwynn Oak and the new demonstration planned for Sunday made her decide it was time for her whole family—kids included—to take a stand against Jim Crow.

Her husband had been planning to take the boys canoeing that Sunday, but she said to him, "Let's take the kids and go get arrested instead." At first he wasn't sure going to the demonstration was a good idea. She managed to change his mind. On Sunday afternoon, they packed everyone into the car and headed to Gwynn Oak. "I had never been to the park before," Tom Coleman recalled. "We knew what it was all about, getting arrested. We knew we weren't going to go on the rides." His brother John added, "I was excited about having an adventure with my parents."

They didn't go to the pre-demonstration rally at Metropolitan Methodist Church. Lu Coleman had received nonviolence training when she first joined CORE and felt she knew what to do. At her earlier training sessions, she said, "They taught us how to cover our heads if attacked and warned us that the first people attacked were the white women because we had betrayed our race by taking part in demonstrations. I knew down South this was a dangerous thing to do," she said. "But I didn't think it would be dangerous in Baltimore. The Fourth of July demonstration at Gwynn Oak was so well organized."

Sunday's demonstration was well organized, too. The Colemans reached the park in late afternoon, around the same time as the protestors who had been at the pre-demonstration rally at the church. "Everyone was so nice and polite," Tom Coleman remembered. "People asked our parents whether we were there to go to the park or to get arrested. They moved us over to the area where people waited to be arrested." Once again, there was a group-by-group plan for the arrests.

Some arrests had already taken place by the time organizers matched the Coleman family up with a black couple. Together, the Colemans and the African American couple walked up to the park entrance, with Mrs. Coleman carrying baby Steve. One of the park's owners stopped them. Professor Coleman said they wanted to protest that blacks "are not admitted to this park." The owner asked the police to arrest them.

A news photographer then snapped the photo that would appear in newspapers the next day, showing a professor, his wife, and their three very young sons being led away to be arrested.

A bus-load full of arrested protestors had just left for the huge Pikesville Armory, which was fairly nearby. Baltimore County officials had learned from the Fourth of July demonstration that the local police station was too small for hordes of arrestees. A temporary detention center had been set up inside the armory for Sunday's event.

Police officers didn't want the Coleman family to have to wait around for another bus to arrive to take them to the armory because of the risk that one of the kids might be injured by the rock-throwing crowd. So officers hurried the Colemans into a police car and sped them off to the armory. "It was fun to ride in a

Professor James Coleman and his son Tom—followed by John and Mrs. Coleman (carrying baby Steve)—walk to a police car after being arrested at Gwynn Oak, July 7, 1963.

Courtesy Baltimore Sun

FACING A HOSTILE CROWD

police car, but I was disappointed not to go with everyone else in the bus," recalled John Coleman.

THE FACE OF HATE

Lu Coleman said her family had been rushed in and out of the park so quickly that she hadn't been aware of the crowd of hecklers and didn't see any rock throwing. She learned about that in the next day's newspapers.

However, other demonstrators at the protest on Sunday were well aware of the boisterous segregationists lined up across the street from Gwynn Oak or standing in a roped-off area inside the park near the front entrance. These Jim Crow supporters had been waiting for nearly four hours in sweltering heat for the protestors to arrive, growing angrier by the minute because the protestors were later than had been expected. Around 5:00 P.M. when the first protestors finally walked up to the front entrance, the hecklers roared with fury and shouted racial slurs and obscenities.

Rev. Bascom and three rabbis were in the first group to be arrested that day. One of the rabbis, Israel Goldman, tried to talk with the park's owners, asking why they had not responded to letters that for years had been sent to them from the Maryland Interracial Commission, of which Rabbi Goldman was vice-chairman. James Price wasn't interested in having a discussion. He asked the police to arrest the rabbi and the others in his group. Once again, some protestors walked to the police vehicles voluntarily after being arrested, but others sat on the ground singing "We Shall Overcome" and had to be carried.

As the arrests proceeded, the white hecklers grew more unruly and threw rocks at the police buses that were headed to the armory. They began pushing up against the rope that held them back. When a few jumped over the rope to try to attack civil rights protestors, Police Chief Robert Lally brought out four K-9 police dogs to patrol in front of the hecklers. The use of the dogs calmed the crowd a bit, but Chief Lally noted, "This is a vicious crowd. One little spark could set 'em off."

One little spark did set off a group of hecklers on the other side of the park. Some protestors decided once again not to follow the group-by-group arrest plan but went around to the back of the park. Alison Turaj Brown, one of these rebels, knew about the back entrance because she had gone to Gwynn Oak as a child. With her were Arthur Waskow, his two SDS friends, and Virginia Lottier Love, a veteran of the Northwood Theatre protests earlier that year. She came with her father, George Lottier, an executive at the *Afro-American* newspaper.

As they waded across the stream at the back of the park, shoes in their hands, a white teenager spotted them. "Hey, you can't come in here," he screamed, flexing a leather belt in his hands, implying that he might use it on them. He shouted for the police, but the protestors kept walking into the park. They stepped across the tracks of the kiddie train and were starting to climb up a hill when a group of angry whites showed up, screaming insults. A middle-aged white woman in a red dress screamed an especially offensive anti-black insult over and over. Then she picked up a rock and threw it at Alison Turaj Brown, knocking off her glasses and cutting two deep gashes over her right eye. Blood streamed down her face, onto her shirt and onto the shirt of Mr. Lottier, who had caught her when she fell. "I was shocked that she did that," said Ms. Brown. "We were scared. We joined hands. We kept moving on."

The angry, screaming mob surrounded them. Arthur Waskow knew from his research on race riots what might happen in such a situation: "First, they yell. Then they throw things and surround you, and then they start beating you up. And then somebody falls and they kill you." As such scary thoughts raced through his mind, police showed up with a police dog and rescued them—by arresting them. "We walked off under arrest, singing 'We Shall Overcome,' with our voices quivering with fear," he said. Ms. Brown told a reporter, "I have seen hate on individual faces, but this is the first time that I have seen group hate."

A news photographer took a photo of five bedraggled protestors, one with blood on her cheek, all with heads bowed, solemnly

AP Photo

On July 7, these Gwynn Oak protestors sang "We Shall Overcome" after being arrested (from left): Arthur Waskow (holding shoes he took off to cross a stream to enter the park), Alison Turaj Brown, Carol McEldowney, Todd Gitlin, Virginia Lottier Love, and George Lottier.

singing the civil rights anthem. A month later, Mr. Waskow wrote an article for the *Saturday Review* magazine in which he said, "I felt utterly pierced by the knowledge that this was my Baltimore, the mob my fellow Baltimoreans, showing me hatred that I had never had to face, but that Baltimore Negroes must have faced for all their lives. . . . I had taken into my guts what I had previously spun out only in my brain: that men were capable of sustained, focused hatred."

Another close call occurred when white teenagers saw two black women enter a restroom. The teens kicked in the restroom door and punched one of the women in the face, only to find that the women were restroom attendants. Newspaper reports about this attack showed the contradiction in allowing dark-skinned people into the park to clean bathrooms but not to ride a merry-go-round.

The restroom attendant wasn't injured badly, but police took Alison Turaj Brown to a hospital to have the gash on her forehead stitched up. Then they arrested her. They never arrested the woman in the red dress who hurled the rock. However, four hecklers were arrested that day, and Chief Lally issued warnings to some of his own officers for being too rough with protestors.

SUNDAY'S TALLY

Ninety-five civil rights protestors were arrested that Sunday, including thirteen local clergymen, one of whom dressed up in a red-white-and-blue Uncle Sam costume to show that he felt protesting was patriotic. In addition to the Colemans, another family group landed in the armory. William Leicht, a biophysics researcher at Johns Hopkins, was taken into custody with his wife and their six-month-old daughter, Cara.

Rodney "Binx" Watts, the 18-year-old son of lawyer Robert Watts, was also arrested at Gwynn Oak that day. He had recently graduated from high school and joined the July 7 protest with a friend. "We had been kind of worried at the beginning of the demonstration," he said. "We didn't know what to expect from the hecklers. When nothing bad happened to us, it was a relief. The police loaded us onto buses and took us to the Pikesville Armory. Inside the armory, it was a joyful, festive occasion. We were singing 'We Shall Overcome' and other protest songs. We felt that we had done something good. We felt that we were making history. Being arrested was a happy experience." Once again, his father worked late into the night, handling legal details for the arrested protestors.

James Williams, a reporter for the *Afro-American*, was also arrested that Sunday. He wrote an article about the day's events for his newspaper. As an arrestee himself, he noted details other reporters missed. For example, on the ride to the armory, the bus driver blared out music over his radio to drown out the protest songs of the demonstrators. He also reported that the police didn't provide food for those under arrest. Protestors inside the armory put money in a paper bag and threw it out a window to supporters outside, who bought food to pass back through the window to

Courtesy Afro-American Newspapers Archives

Afro-American reporter James Williams (center, in jacket) sings protest songs with others who were arrested with him at Gwynn Oak on July 7, 1963.

hungry protestors inside. The food-delivery system amazed Binx Watts, who recalled later that "people were literally throwing hamburgers to us through the windows of the armory."

Several ministers and Mr. Williams wanted to spend the night in jail, but police refused to let protestors fill the jails, as they had on the Fourth of July. Most protestors were released without having to pay bail, as long as they agreed to return on Wednesday for a court hearing.

Mr. Williams was especially moved by seeing the Coleman and Leicht families with their young kids in the armory, "upholding the finest traditions of this land." He was upset that the families didn't get to leave until after midnight, having been made to wait until after nearly everyone else was booked. "I wondered whether they were punishing us for bringing our children," said Lu Coleman. "Well, it was no punishment for my children. The baby slept, and the two older ones had the greatest time, being able to stay

JAILBIRD

James D. Williams, an *Afro-American* newspaper writer, decided to be arrested with protestors at Gwynn Oak on July 7, 1963. In an article in the paper two days later, he explained why: "There comes a time in life when one can no longer sit on the sidelines while others fight his battles. . . . Under a warm and almost cloudless sky and the dark glances and darker words of a mob, we went to jail for entering Gwynn Oak Park. Compared to what others have and are doing, this took but little courage—but this act, in its way, will help bring an end to all this crazy race madness . . . I am glad that I am now a jailbird."

up all night. People brought in food for them, hot dogs, hamburgers, milk shakes." After a while, eight-year-old Tom fell asleep on a bench, but his brother John stayed up and noted later, "I watched all the people get fingerprinted, including our parents. That was a little upsetting, to see them fingerprinted." He wasn't fingerprinted because the kids were too young to actually be arrested. Tom Coleman said he felt "really proud. Gwynn Oak was a huge event for us and we realized the political significance of it. I remember being a little disappointed that it wasn't more of an event. The actual arrest was so efficient and low key, a little bit of a letdown that it wasn't more exciting. But we were pleased to be part of something that we thought was the right thing to do."

PHOTO POWER

The next day, there were long articles about the demonstration, not only in Baltimore newspapers but in the *New York Times* and other out-of-town papers. Some stories included the photo of the Coleman family being arrested. Other news reports included the picture of a bleeding Alison Turaj Brown and her small band of rebel protestors. Both of these photos showed scenes Baltimoreans might expect to see from a protest in the Deep South, but not in their supposedly more progressive city. Those images, along with another that showed a rabbi being fingerprinted, may have helped tip the balance, leading more people to decide that enough was enough. It was time for Gwynn Oak to change.

A different photograph in the *Afro-American* newspaper made another point about Jim Crow—how ridiculous it was. This front-page photo showed a smiling 11-year-old, Lydia Phinney Wilkins, and her aunt, Mabel Grant, who had gone on an undercover mission at Gwynn Oak that Sunday.

"Our family comes in different shades," explained Lydia Phinney Wilkins, who like her aunt has light-colored skin. "Growing up, I knew I was black, but other people didn't always know." An editor at the *Afro-American* newspaper asked Mrs. Grant to go to Gwynn Oak on the morning of July 7 before the protest started and join the crowd of white customers standing in line to buy tickets. Maybe the ticket-takers would be so busy worrying about the demonstration that they wouldn't notice that she was actually African American. After all, many other customers with their summer tans would probably have darker skin tones than Mrs. Grant. The newspaper had pulled pranks on Jim Crow businesses before. In 1961, reporters put on African robes, entered a Jim Crow restaurant and were served, thus pointing out how ridiculous it was for a restaurant to serve dark-skinned people if they were Africans but not if they were African Americans.

Mrs. Grant was a teacher who, with her husband, Dr. James Preston Grant, Jr., had been a big supporter of efforts to end Jim Crow. She had taken her daughter to hear Dr. King when he spoke at the 1961 civil rights conference in Baltimore. Mrs. Grant had a spirit of adventure and agreed to the plan, but she thought it would be easier to slip into the park with a child. Her 13-year-old daughter, Linda, wanted to join her. "I was younger than the college students who were doing the Freedom Rides and lunch counter sit-ins. I'd been seeing them on the news each night and had the greatest admiration for them," said Linda Grant. "When the *Afro* approached my mother about Gwynn Oak, I said, 'I want

COSTLY PHOTO

Robert Moore, a Morgan freshman in 1963, had been on some demonstrations with the Baltimore NAACP's youth group, but he longed to do something more adventurous, like the Freedom Riders he heard about during high school. So on July 7, 1963, he joined in when his church's minister asked for volunteers to head over to Gwynn Oak after Sunday service. A photo of him being arrested at Gwynn Oak appeared in a newspaper the next day, causing him to lose his summer job at a car wash. That didn't keep this new activist from joining future protests. Years later, he became an important Baltimore union leader.

to go.' But my mother said, 'You know, we're going to take your cousin Lydia instead because she is lighter than you.' I understood exactly why. The point was to show that skin color is the worst reason to evaluate people."

Like the Coleman boys, Lydia Phinney Wilkins didn't know kids of other races. Young kids generally went to their neighborhood elementary school. If no white kids lived in the neighborhood, as was true of hers, there would be no white kids at the school. She had also never been to an amusement park. "I knew we weren't supposed to go to Gwynn Oak, but I didn't really understand why." She didn't think her parents were trying to protect her from learning about Jim Crow. "It was just a lack of awareness," she said. "My neighborhood was all that I knew. Aunt Mabel was fun. She said we were going to the park. I thought it would be fun." And it was.

"We walked right in and enjoyed the day. Nobody noticed," said Mrs. Grant. Her niece recalled, "The people were nice to us. Nobody was mean. The park was huge and it was so crowded." During their two-hour visit, they ate at the snack bar and rode on the Ferris wheel and merry-go-round. They heard park workers talking about the upcoming demonstration, saying that it was

The front page of the Afro-American newspaper, July 9, 1963, with a photo of Mabel Grant and her niece, Lydia Phinney Wilkins, African Americans who slipped into the park before the July 7 Gwynn Oak protest began.

Courtesy Afro-American Newspapers Archives

important not to let in African Americans. "I had to smile when they said we wouldn't get in since we were in," said Mrs. Grant. Shortly after hearing those remarks, she and her niece left the park. Mrs. Grant's conclusion about Gwynn Oak's Jim Crow policy: "It was so absurd."

The photo of Lydia Phinney Wilkins in the *Afro-American* and the accompanying article made the point that nothing terrible happened at Gwynn Oak because two African Americans went on the rides. The newspaper got her name wrong, but that didn't bother her. "I know it was me. My family was glad to see that it was me," she said. "Years later, I realized the significance of my going to the park and how dangerous it could have been." Even so, she thinks it was the right thing to do.

The Ad Hoc Committee to Desegregate Gwynn Oak was ready to call for another demonstration. But perhaps enough people had by then reached the same conclusion as Mrs. Grant about the park's absurd policy. Perhaps Baltimore County officials would pressure the Price brothers to negotiate an end to the crisis.

"We reluctantly agreed to break the letter of the law in order to direct the attention of the faithful to the tragic gap between ideal and practice in our democracy."

—Baltimore Interfaith Committee, July 6, 1963

© James Singewald

A WAR OF WORDS

1963

A HEATED WAR OF WORDS broke out the day after Sunday's demonstration. Firing the first salvo was Spiro T. Agnew, the top elected official in Baltimore County. A few years later, he became Maryland's governor. In 1969 he became the country's vice president, but had to resign in 1973, the first vice president ever forced to leave office because of criminal corruption charges.

Those troubles were in the future. On Monday, July 8, 1963, his focus was Gwynn Oak Amusement Park. Mr. Agnew had caused a stir by declaring that Sunday's Gwynn Oak demonstrators were "wasting taxpayers' money." He called the demonstrators "hasty and immature and victims of self-hypnosis." Perhaps he was annoyed that protest leaders had ignored his request to cancel Sunday's demonstration. He may also have been irritated that the Ad Hoc Committee to Desegregate Gwynn Oak Park had already announced that there would be yet another demonstration coming up on Tuesday.

Things calmed down after Mr. Agnew met on Monday with a small group of those he had just called "hasty and immature," including Baltimore County activist Eugene King, the NAACP's Juanita Jackson Mitchell, Rev. Marion C. Bascom, and other members of the Ad Hoc Committee. They explained to Mr. Agnew the importance to the black community of the nearly ten-year-long effort to end discrimination at Gwynn Oak, hardly a new or "hasty" undertaking. Mr. Agnew persuaded them that he really was committed to ending segregation. After the meeting, the black leaders issued a statement saying they were impressed with Mr. Agnew's "sincerity," while also stating quite firmly that Sunday's demonstration had not been "hasty and immature."

Another verbal blast came from the Maryland Commission on Interracial Problems and Relations. On Monday, this commission sent Gwynn Oak's owners a letter, which also appeared in local newspapers. The letter described segregation at Gwynn Oak as un-American and rejected the owners' fears of economic suicide: "There is an abundance of evidence to prove that the lowering of racial barriers enhances business profits." The letter claimed that Gwynn Oak was harming Maryland's image. "Is the desire to protect personal racial prejudice paramount to love of State and nation? Is the prestige of 'lily-white' Gwynn Oak Park of greater moment than the prestige of the State of Maryland?"

The Ad Hoc Committee to Desegregate Gwynn Oak Park fired off letters, too. One went to U.S. Attorney General Robert Kennedy, urging him to become involved. The Ad Hoc Committee also sent a letter to Governor J. Millard Tawes, asking him to have state police officers patrol Gwynn Oak.

By Monday evening, the Baltimore County Council had at last created the promised Baltimore County Human Relations Commission. Its first job: End the Gwynn Oak crisis.

OPENING MOVES

CORE helped get negotiations going by announcing on Tuesday that it was canceling that day's demonstration, but warned that plans were underway for a demonstration on Saturday.

Spiro Agnew met separately with both sides on Tuesday: first with James and David Price, two of the park's owners, and then with several civil rights leaders. "I don't think I can say we have

Adah Jenkins, picketing the police station where hearings were held for those arrested during the July 1963 protests at Gwynn Oak.

Courtesy Afro-American Newspapers Archives

changed each others' opinions to any major degree," Mr. Agnew said of the meetings. Both sides agreed to meet with the new Human Relations Commission for a negotiating session on Friday afternoon.

Mr. Agnew tried to persuade CORE to give in on two key points before Friday's negotiations. First, he asked CORE to call a longer halt to more demonstrations. He also asked CORE to agree that future demonstrations would involve picketing only, no mass arrests. Ed Chance was willing to delay having more demonstrations if negotiations went well, "if we can see reasonable signs of progress." But he rejected the no-mass-arrests request. So did

Rabbi Israel Goldman, a member of the Ad Hoc Committee, who said, "We're interested in pressuring Gwynn Oak Park . . . we're interested in stirring public opinion. Sometimes people in government have a way of dragging their feet." Mass arrests created the crisis that forced county officials to start the negotiations. Without the threat of more arrests, foot dragging was likely.

Mr. Agnew said there was nothing he could do officially to end segregation at Gwynn Oak because only the state legislature could pass a law requiring amusement parks to integrate. But he signaled to Gwynn Oak's owners the move he hoped they would make by saying, "Morally I feel that the park should be integrated."

Pressure on the park's owners came from other sources as well. An editorial in the *Sun* challenged the Price brothers' argument that they had the right to admit whomever they pleased. The editorial noted that if a business opens its doors to serve the public, it should serve all members of the public. Pressure even came from the U.S. Senate, where Senator Hubert Humphrey of Minnesota called the arrests at Gwynn Oak a "flagrant abuse" of the Constitution. This Senate leader would become the nation's vice president in 1965. In his Senate speech about Gwynn Oak, he said the arrests showed why Congress needed to pass a law to end segregation in all such businesses. Yet another form of pressure came from rumors that movie star Marlon Brando might join future Gwynn Oak protests.

But the pressure that probably made the biggest impression on the Price brothers came from their own ticket booths. James Price told a *Sun* reporter that, since the protests started that summer, business was down.

TALKS BEGIN

The negotiating session on Friday, July 12, brought together members of the Baltimore County Human Relations Commission, the Price brothers, and representatives of the Ad Hoc Committee to Desegregate Gwynn Oak Park. At the end of that day's discussion, the commission offered its first proposal: Gwynn Oak should integrate by July 26. The Price brothers had until the next negotiation meeting on Monday afternoon to decide whether to accept the July 26 deadline.

To give the Prices time to think, protest leaders canceled Saturday's demonstration, but they let it be known that they had other options. They announced that civil rights leaders would meet privately with Governor Tawes on Monday, a few hours before the start of the next negotiation session. The governor was no doubt eager to see the Gwynn Oak situation solved because he had his hands full dealing with violence that had flared up again in Cambridge, Maryland, in connection with civil rights sit-ins there.

At Monday's negotiation session, the Price brothers rejected the idea of integrating the park by July 26. They also managed to inflame the situation by using language that was offensive to the people with whom they were supposed to be negotiating. First, they described the July 26 proposal as "an ultimatum" and as "an economic lynching party," insensitive wording to use with so many African Americans in the room. Then the Price brothers invited a minister from a church near Gwynn Oak to give a speech in which he compared the demonstrators to followers of Hitler. Many found that comparison insulting, especially the Jewish members of the Ad Hoc Committee. About ten people—both black and white—walked out of the room at that point.

Commission members suggested a new proposal: Wait until the next year to integrate Gwynn Oak. The Price brothers liked that idea, but protest leaders turned it down, saying the park had to integrate before the end of the summer. James Price countered that integrating so soon meant he would lose a lot of white customers, especially ones who had already made reservations to have parties and picnics at Gwynn Oak and might not like the idea of an integrated park.

However, Mr. Price also noted, "We have not slammed the door on negotiations." A new negotiation session was set for three days later, on Thursday evening, July 18. Once again, protest leaders agreed not to hold any demonstrations in the meantime.

Courtesy Baltimore Sun

News photos, such as this one of Rev. Jack Malpas, minister of an Episcopal church located not far from Gwynn Oak, helped turn public opinion against segregation at Gwynn Oak.

Debate about Gwynn Oak was also taking place on local TV programs and on the Letters to the Editor page of the *Sun*. Some people wrote to the *Sun* to condemn the clergy for breaking the Trespass Law and being arrested, using strong words such as "disgusting" and "repulsive" to criticize the religious leaders' actions. One letter-writer claimed that private property rights were as important as "life itself." In addition to these letters to the *Sun*, some priests who took part in the CORE protests at Gwynn Oak received hostile letters from their own parishioners who were angry about what the priests had done. But other letters printed in the *Sun* congratulated the clergy for "their obedience to a higher law." One letter-writer noted, "It is disappointing to find so many Americans who have forgotten our tradition of civil disobedience that began with the Boston Tea Party." Another, who said he was white, wrote in to warn that if segregation continued, "prejudices will increase and harden and hatred will prevail for future generations. We will become a divided nation, disorganized and weakened by civil strife."

MARATHON SESSION

On Thursday, July 18, before the next negotiating session began, civil rights leaders offered a new proposal to members of the Baltimore County Human Relations Commission. The protest leaders suggested that Gwynn Oak should integrate on the first day of August, but added that the park could close to the public whenever parties or picnics had been scheduled by groups that objected to integration. This compromise could help lessen the Price brothers' fears about losing money. But there was a catch: The protest leaders set a deadline. If the Price brothers didn't accept this proposal by noon on Friday, there would be a huge demonstration on Saturday with mass arrests.

That evening, as the negotiation session began, commission members presented the protest leaders' new offer to the Price brothers. There were rumors, however, that a group of more radical demonstrators, led by 21-year-old Leo Burroughs, Jr., planned to demonstrate on Saturday no matter what happened in the negotiations. Rev. Robert T. Newbold, Jr., a member of the Ad Hoc Committee to Desegregate Gwynn Oak Park, said his group might not be able to control those more hot-headed protestors if there was more delay in reaching an agreement. He explained, "The longer the problem remains unresolved, the more difficult it becomes to exercise this kind of control." This worried the chairman of the county's Human Relations Commission. He feared that more protests might lead to "possible bloodshed."

That evening's negotiating session lasted eight hours, ending early the following morning. At the start of that marathon session, everyone agreed on one thing: Gwynn Oak Park would be integrated. The question was: When?

Throughout that evening's negotiations, different dates were suggested and rejected. The Price brothers wanted September. No way, said the civil rights leaders. Waiting until after school started meant few black youngsters would have a chance to visit the park. Rabbi Abraham Shusterman, a Human Relations Commission member, suggested August 15. David Price rejected any August date, using another unfortunate word choice, by saying, "We are in the business of selling entertainment, not holocaust."

Wiser words came from Father Joseph Connolly, the priest who had brought so many members of his parish to the July 7 protest. An impassioned speech by Father Connolly helped focus the discussion. He urged his fellow whites at the negotiating table to realize how important the desire for equal rights was to the black community. He pleaded, "You all don't know the urgency of this situation. I have screamed at the Governor. I have screamed to the Archbishop. I have challenged my Archbishop by getting a priest arrested. How can I make you understand?"

Father Connolly offered a suggestion that he hoped would provide the key to reaching a settlement. He promised that he and other clergy would find groups to book events at Gwynn Oak in order to replace any organizations that might cancel reservations because of integration. He said local clergy would do all they could to encourage people to keep going to Gwynn Oak.

Courtesy Hearst Corporation

Picketers outside the police station where arrested Gwynn Oak protestors had been taken.

This suggestion didn't produce an agreement by the time the exhausted negotiators went home on Friday morning at about 4:00 A.M. But the pledge of future bookings planted the idea that integration might not lead to economic suicide after all. As Rev. Bascom noted, "Money is the name of the game."

A LONG TIME COMING

On Friday morning, July 19, there was still no settlement, but there was a real possibility that CORE would hold another huge demonstration at Gwynn Oak the next day. Several local organizations had promised to provide lots of volunteers for such a protest.

NEW MINDSET

In 1965, Robert Bell was a Morgan senior and was worried that his 1960 arrest at Hooper's Restaurant might keep him from getting into Harvard Law School. By then, Maryland's Court of Appeals had overturned his conviction, but Harvard's application asked about any arrests. "I didn't know what the impact of that arrest would be when they started to review my application," he said. "As it turned out, it was not a negative at all. It was a plus. That's a tribute to the way we have changed. Once people began to have a changed mindset, they looked on activities that made the change possible as favorable as opposed to negative. People realized it was the right thing to do." In 1996, this Harvard Law graduate became the first African American chief judge on the same Court of Appeals that overturned his sit-in conviction.

County office workers were swamped typing up court documents for the nearly 400 protestors who had been arrested on July 4 and 7. More arrests would be a disaster, not only for the office staff, but also for the image of Baltimore County. It was trying to build its business community and didn't want more negative publicity. Spiro Agnew, Baltimore County's chief executive, was determined to prevent Saturday's demonstration.

All day Friday, Mr. Agnew carried out a nonstop campaign of telephone diplomacy, switching back and forth between speaking with the Price brothers and with protest leaders. James Price told a *New York Times* reporter that pressure on him to compromise came from all directions, including from other business people, as well as from religious leaders, government officials, and of course, civil rights activists.

Finally, late that Friday night, July 19, just two weeks and a day after the big Fourth of July showdown, the telephone negotiations came to an end. Shortly before midnight, Mr. Agnew brought all the interested parties together in a county office building. He announced that at last there was an agreement, one that he said was "a good example for the state." The agreement provided that:

* Segregation would end at Gwynn Oak on August 28, 1963, giving both sides part of what they wanted—an August date to please the protest leaders, but one that was almost September, to please the park's owners.
* The Price brothers would ask county officials to drop arrest charges against all protestors.
* Civil rights leaders promised to have no more demonstrations at Gwynn Oak.

After nearly ten years, Jim Crow would no longer hold the reins of power at Gwynn Oak Amusement Park. Finally, children of any background would have the right to step right up, buy a ticket, climb into the saddle of a carousel horse, and ride round and round on a beautiful merry-go-round. The pain of being excluded because of skin color would now be banished from one more aspect of daily life in the Baltimore area.

Dr. King had worried that being excluded, even from an amusement park, might cause "depressing clouds of inferiority" to form in the "mental sky" of African American youngsters, as he noted in his 1963 *Letter from Birmingham City Jail.* The Supreme Court had also worried about the psychological damage that such exclusion could cause youngsters' "hearts and minds," as noted in the 1954 *Brown v. Board of Education* school decision. The Gwynn Oak agreement officially ended that kind of exclusion, at least at this amusement park. The agreement also created the possibility that kids—both black and white—might have a chance now to learn something from the experience of riding side by side with youngsters of different backgrounds, having fun together, perhaps even learning a bit about how to get along together. These were important skills for a multicultural society with many more problems to solve.

Figuring out how to knock Jim Crow out of the saddle at Gwynn Oak had involved a long, hard learning process to find the right

HAIRSPRAY

Tilted Acres, the amusement park in the first *Hairspray* movie, is based on Gwynn Oak. John Waters, who wrote the film, grew up in Baltimore. He made up most of the events in the movie, but there really was a TV dance show similar to the one in *Hairspray*. The real *Buddy Deane Show* was whites-only, except one day a month when it was blacks-only. In 1962, CIG held a protest against the segregated show, and an interracial "dance-in" took place the next year, organized by Gwynn Oak protestor Danny Schechter and his Northern Student Movement boss, Bill Henry. They arranged for black teens to be on the show on August 12, 1963. As the teens entered the studio, college-age whites rushed in, too. They all danced together, live on TV. In *Hairspray*, the show integrates. In real life, the TV station received bomb threats and hate mail because of the interracial dance-in. The station decided to cancel the *Buddy Deane Show* in 1964.

mix of tactics: mass arrests and massive publicity, economic pressure, and moral persuasion—backed up by solid, organizational ground work and with a tantalizing promise of future bookings to sweeten the deal.

Victory required a joint effort by all the groups that had protested against Jim Crow in Baltimore for so long: the NAACP and Urban League, CORE, CIG, as well as churches, synagogues, and other sympathetic organizations. They might have philosophical differences, but as Charles Mason noted, "On a large demonstration, the groups worked together."

Even the young civil rights firebrands who had planned to demonstrate—no matter what—at Gwynn Oak on Saturday, July 20, agreed not to do so. They had already played an important role in helping to force a settlement simply by *threatening* to demonstrate. Five of them actually showed up to protest at Gwynn Oak that Saturday, the day after the agreement had been reached, but they went home when urged to do so by Father Connolly and Rev. Wickwire.

A few members of the segregationist group F.A.N. picketed at the park that Saturday, hoping to start a white boycott of the integrated Gwynn Oak. Their plans fizzled. Baltimore was ready to move on.

Soon the park's beautiful merry-go-round would move on as well, onto the pages of history, when a little girl in a pink dress settled into the saddle of one of its jaunty horses.

"I hope people of both races continue to support the park."

—Charles Langley, August 28, 1963

Courtesy Baltimore Sun

A DREAM TO KEEP
WORKING ON
1963 and Beyond

"MY FIRST SHOCK WAS when I saw the reporters," said Marian Langley. She was describing what it felt like when her family became the first African Americans to enter Gwynn Oak on Wednesday, August 28, 1963, the start of a new era at this amusement park.

She and her husband, Charles, had thought about going to Washington that day, to be part of the huge crowd gathering there for the March on Washington for Jobs and Freedom, at which Dr. King would give his "I Have a Dream" speech. They couldn't find a baby-sitter for their 11-month-old daughter, Sharon, and decided that a big civil rights rally wouldn't be a great place for a toddler. Mr. Langley had an official March on Washington button pinned to his jacket when he arrived at Gwynn Oak. The button showed a handshake between a black hand and a white one.

Facing page: Sharon Langley with her father, Charles C. Langley, Jr., at Gwynn Oak Amusement Park, August 28, 1963.

A March on Washington button.

The Langleys hadn't gone to any of that summer's demonstrations at Gwynn Oak, but they had read about them in newspapers and knew the park would be open to all for the first time on August 28. They were fairly new to Baltimore, having moved there four years earlier, but they weren't new to the civil rights struggle. Mrs. Langley had taken a stand against Jim Crow as a teenager in the late 1950s when she helped integrate the high school that served her Georgetown, Kentucky, hometown. She had been hoping to go to college, but there weren't enough college prep classes at her town's segregated one-room schoolhouse for black students. She made a request to go to the newer high school that whites attended. At first, local officials refused and paid instead to bus her to a larger, better-equipped black high school in the nearby city of Lexington. Soon so many others in her town asked to do the same thing that officials decided it would cost less to let them go to the town's white high school, which was actually closer to her home than the segregated school.

During the summer of 1963, Mrs. Langley was working as a nurse at a Baltimore hospital while also taking college classes. She had to be on duty at the hospital later in the day on August 28. She and her husband decided to squeeze in a visit to Gwynn Oak before she had to go to work, to give their daughter her first amusement park experience. Mr. Langley had the day off from his job as a clerk at the Social Security Administration office, located not far from Gwynn Oak. Federal offices in the Baltimore and Washington area were closed. Having fewer people on the streets going to work would make it easier for D.C. police to deal with any disturbances that might occur during the Washington demonstration. For the same reason, the Washington Senators baseball team called off a home game with the Minnesota Twins that was scheduled for that day.

"GLAD WE CAME"

As soon as the Langley family entered the park, reporters and photographers surrounded them, snapping photos and asking how the parents felt on this historic day. "I don't feel funny or odd or anything," Mrs. Langley said, noting that she didn't "approach it

Courtesy Hearst Corporation

Sharon Langley with her father.

with hostility." She added, "The man said it's open and we took him at face value."

The family strolled around for a while, checking out the arcade games, and then made their way over to the merry-go-round. Mrs. Langley waited off to the side as her husband carried Sharon on-board and picked a row of brightly colored horses for his daughter's first spin on a merry-go-round. He perched his daughter in the saddle of a dappled horse, keeping a firm grip on her so she wouldn't fall. He planned to stay on the ride with her because she was too little to hold on by herself.

Two white youngsters about age six—a boy and a girl—climbed onto horses on either side of Sharon. They were big enough to ride by themselves, but the girl's mother asked Mr. Langley to keep an eye on her daughter to make sure the little girl would be safe during the ride. He was glad to help. This perfectly normal parent-to-parent request—so typical of the way parents help each other at playgrounds and parks—took on special meaning this day. "These are the kinds of things that make me feel we'll be accepted," he told a reporter later.

When Sharon's horse began to move up and down, her eyes grew wide with wonder—or perhaps a touch of fear. Her dad was there to keep her safe, and her two fellow riders as well. All three youngsters had fun that afternoon riding round and round together.

The Langleys' history-making visit lasted a little less than an hour. A short visit—and a quiet one—but an important one nonetheless, showing by its lack of drama just how dramatically different things were. Throughout the afternoon, a few other African American families visited the park and enjoyed spins on the Ferris wheel and other attractions. Before arriving, none of these families had been sure that they would be made to feel welcome. The day turned out fine. Many white families were there, too. No fights broke out. No rocks were hurled or insults shouted. It was a peaceful day at the park, as visits to an amusement park are supposed to be.

Mr. Langley told a reporter that he planned to come back to Gwynn Oak, especially the next week when a veterans group was

Other African American visitors to Gwynn Oak on August 28, 1963.

Courtesy Hearst Corporation

holding a picnic there. "I hope people of both races continue to support the park. I see no reason why it shouldn't be a tremendous success." He and his wife concluded, "We're glad we came."

David Price, one of the park's owners, was glad, too, telling a reporter, "I am very pleased with the type of people who came." Not as many African American families showed up as he had expected, but he figured that was because so many were either at the March on Washington or home watching it on TV. He noted that he was happy that clergy and other community leaders had found groups to hold parties and picnics at the park, following up on the promise Father Connolly had made at the last negotiation session. On the morning of August 28, an article in the *Sun* reported that the head of the Baltimore County Human Relations Commission planned to come to Gwynn Oak and hoped others would, too. In that same article, Rev. Marion C. Bascom urged people to visit Gwynn Oak "to give the Price brothers the cooperation they deserve."

The day after the Langley family visited the park, the *Sun* featured a photo and story about their Gwynn Oak excursion. Stories appeared in other papers, including the *New York Times* and *Washington Post*. News articles emphasized the striking contrast between the turmoil that had gripped the park eight weeks earlier and the peaceful atmosphere the Langleys found there.

A MIGHTY MARCH

Of course, newspapers were also filled with reports about the March on Washington for Jobs and Freedom, which had been an amazing success. More than 200,000 demonstrators—white and black—filled the area in front of the Lincoln Memorial to hear Dr. King and others call for economic opportunity for all and an end to injustice. There had been rumors that members of the American Nazi Party would be there, too, and that they and mobs of other segregationists might cause trouble. But the march was peaceful, with no major disruptions.

There were no mass arrests either. March organizers decided that arrests weren't necessary for this event. A huge, orderly crowd—the largest ever to come to a civil rights rally—would be newsworthy enough to make the point that a great many Americans were fed up with Jim Crow.

Rev. Dr. Eugene Carson Blake, who had been arrested at Gwynn Oak in July, was an official speaker at the event, one of several who addressed the crowd before Dr. King spoke. Catholic and Jewish clergy also spoke that day, as did the national leaders of civil rights organizations: Whitney Young of the Urban League, Roy Wilkins of the NAACP, and John Lewis of SNCC. It was a day for people to come together for a common cause.

About 8,000 Marylanders traveled by car or bus to be part of the March on Washington. Walter Carter had organized Maryland's participation, assisted by other Baltimoreans, including Charles Mason, who noted, "That was the largest event we had

The huge crowd that came to the March on Washington, as seen from the Lincoln Memorial, where Dr. King spoke.

Rev. Dr. Martin Luther King, Jr. (toward left end, front row) at the March on Washington—at the other end of the row, in a dark jacket and straw hat is Rev. Dr. Eugene Carson Blake.

ever organized." Many who had protested at Gwynn Oak in July went to the march. Some even stopped by Gwynn Oak on their way home.

Linda Grant would have liked to have been at the march, too. "I was annoyed that my parents wouldn't let me go," she said. Her mother, Mabel Grant, had gone on that undercover mission at Gwynn Oak with 11-year-old Lydia Phinney Wilkins right before the July 7 protest. Mrs. Grant feared there might be violence in Washington and thought a safer place for 13-year-old Linda to see history being made was in front of a TV set. "But the march was so peaceful," said Linda Grant. "I said to my parents, 'I told you so.'"

James Farmer, CORE's national director, also saw the Washington rally on TV—from a jail in Louisiana where he had recently been arrested during a demonstration. He was supposed to be at the March on Washington, giving a speech along with other national civil rights leaders. Instead, he sent his speech to another CORE official, Floyd McKissick, who read it aloud to the crowd gathered at the Lincoln Memorial.

Another TV viewer that day was President Kennedy, who stayed in the White House but watched the broadcast of the speeches taking place at the Lincoln Memorial. After the rally ended, he met at the White House with Dr. King and other march leaders. The president issued a statement that said: "We have witnessed today in Washington tens of thousands of Americans—both Negro and white—exercising their right to assemble peaceably and direct the widest possible attention to a great national issue. . . . this Nation can properly be proud of the demonstration that has occurred here today."

KEEPING UP THE PRESSURE

The Gywnn Oak victory and the March on Washington were major achievements, but Baltimore CORE members weren't taking it easy. No sooner had a Gwynn Oak agreement been reached, than Baltimore CORE began organizing protests at other businesses in the area that still had Jim Crow rules, such as private swimming clubs and bowling alleys. They also began protesting discrimination in employment and housing. In addition, the NAACP and other concerned Baltimoreans kept trying to prod the Maryland legislature to pass a public accommodations law that would cover the whole state.

Dr. King's Southern Christian Leadership Conference was busy, too, planning more demonstrations. Jim Crow remained strong in many Southern states. Civil rights leaders continued trying to persuade Congress to pass laws to end segregation everywhere. One of the most active of these persuaders was Juanita Jackson Mitchell's husband, Clarence Mitchell, Jr., the NAACP's chief lobbyist in Washington, often referred to as the "101st Senator."

The road forward was rough. A few weeks after the March on Washington, violence broke out in Alabama over efforts to

Courtesy Hearst Corporation

This Baltimore church was a staging area for buses taking people to the March on Washington on August 28, 1963.

integrate Birmingham's schools; four black girls were killed when their Birmingham church was bombed. Other shocking episodes of violence followed. On November 22, 1963, an assassin shot and killed President Kennedy. His death rocked the nation. He had recently spoken eloquently of the need for civil rights legislation, giving people hope that an official end to segregation might soon be possible. But during the summer after his death, the brutal murder of three civil rights workers in the South showed yet again how entrenched the Jim Crow system still was. Those three young men—two whites and one black—were killed in Mississippi in June 1964 for trying to register African Americans to vote. One of the murdered civil rights workers, 23-year-old CORE volunteer Michael Schwerner, had been at Gwynn Oak Amusement Park the previous summer, taking part in the Fourth of July protest.

In St. Augustine, Florida, protests during the spring of 1964 resulted in mass arrests. Dr. King was arrested there in June. News photos from Florida—combined with all the shocking photos from other demonstrations that had been filling newspapers for about a decade—helped persuade enough lawmakers that it was time to act. In addition, many of them wanted to honor the memory of slain President Kennedy by supporting the civil rights legislation he had backed.

At long last, important laws were passed in 1964 that ended key parts of the Jim Crow system. First, during the spring, Maryland's legislature passed a new statewide public accommodations law that was more far-reaching than the one it had passed the year before. Then the U.S. Congress passed the Civil Rights Act of 1964, which ended Jim Crow in hotels, restaurants, theaters, stores, amusement parks, and all other places that served the public anywhere in the United States. President Lyndon Johnson signed the bill into law on July 2, 1964, almost exactly one year after the Fourth of July showdown at Gwynn Oak.

However, that nationwide 1964 law didn't end voting rights abuses. Civil rights leaders organized huge voting rights demonstrations during March 1965 in Selma, Alabama. Several Gwynn Oak veterans joined the Selma marches, including Rev. Marion C. Bascom, Rev. Vernon Dobson, Father Joseph Connolly, and Rev. William Sloan Coffin. News reports of police brutality in Selma led Congress to pass the Voting Rights Act of 1965, striking down state laws that made it hard for African Americans to vote.

CHALLENGES CONTINUE

Despite the passage of those new laws, the battle for equal rights wasn't over—and, many say, still isn't over. More demonstrations would take place over the following years to open up more opportunity for everyone in jobs, housing, electoral politics, and education.

ANOTHER AUGUST DAY

On August 28, 2008—forty-five years after Dr. King gave his famous speech—an African American senator from Illinois accepted his party's nomination to run for president. Less than three months later, that candidate, Barack Obama, was elected, becoming the first African American to be president of the United States. "It's amazing," said Lu Coleman. "I'm so thrilled to think that in 1963 we were arrested for trying to go into an amusement park with a black couple and then in 2009 there's a black couple living in the White House."

During the late 1960s and early 1970s, the nature of the civil rights movement changed. Some things stayed the same: The NAACP and Urban League kept doing what they had always done—extend and expand upon gains that had already been made. Dr. King remained as committed as ever to nonviolent resistance, although his focus widened to include economic, employment, housing, and anti-war issues. But some groups, including CORE, turned away from a commitment to interracial, nonviolent protest, adopting a more confrontational approach that went by the name Black Power. Its symbol was a raised, clenched, black fist. James Farmer stepped down as CORE's national director in 1966. Some longtime Baltimore CORE members drifted away from the new, more militant CORE and found other ways to keep working for social and economic justice.

In April 1968, Baltimore, like some other American cities, experienced several days of rioting as some in the African American community reacted with fury when Dr. King was killed in Memphis, Tennessee. He had gone there to support sanitation workers who were on strike, asking for better treatment and more opportunities. After the 1968 tragedy of Dr. King's death, a long period of healing followed in Baltimore. Community leaders—black and white—worked to restore peace and tried to create more job-training, employment, and housing opportunities for those who were struggling. Many people who had worked to open up Gwynn Oak played major roles in restoring calm after Dr. King's assassination and looked for ways to revitalize the city during the late 1960s and early 1970s.

Baltimore still faces challenges, but now there is a wider range of people trying to find solutions. No longer are African Americans shut out of the decision-making process, but instead hold high leadership positions, not only in city government, but also in Baltimore's educational and judicial systems, as well as in its legal, artistic, and business communities. Judge Bell noted that there is still work to be done, observing that although places where people work are generally integrated, there is not as much racial integration in Baltimore's residential neighborhoods or in its schools. Even so, the city has come a long way from the Jim Crow days of 1947 when only white youngsters could take a ride on Gwynn Oak's brand new merry-go-round.

The merry-go-round has come a long way, too. After spending a quarter of a century in a small, old-time Trolley Park, it moved to its new, prized position in the heart of the nation's capital, a change brought about not by protestors but by a powerful force of nature.

"Courage, after all, is not being unafraid, but doing what needs to be done in spite of fear."

—James Farmer, from his autobiography,
Lay Bare the Heart, 1985

© James Singewald

MOVING ON

" GWYNN PARK INTEGRATION Called Financial Success."
That headline in the September 14, 1963, *Washington Post*
showed that Gwynn Oak had not committed economic suicide by
integrating. The newspaper reported that the park earned more
money the first weekend in September 1963 than it had on the
same weekend the year before. "There has been no disorder," said
Arthur Price, Jr., in a *Sun* article. "We have gone out of our way to
make the Negroes welcome." Many groups that had been boycotting the park returned as customers and even made reservations
to have outings at the park the next year. "We are thankful to the
people of our community for their help," said Mr. Price. "The future to me is bright."

Gwynn Oak held its first All Nations Day Festival of the post–
Jim Crow era in late September 1963. At long last, two nations with
largely black populations were invited, Jamaica and Trinidad. A
steel band from Trinidad won a prize for its lively music. Another
sign of change: The benediction for the festival was given by Rev.
Frank Williams, the minster at the church where protestors had

*Facing page: In 1996, this sea dragon joined the old Gwynn Oak merry-go-
round in its new home on the National Mall.*

assembled for pre-demonstration rallies before the two huge protests that rocked Gwynn Oak less than three months before.

At the start of the next summer season, James Price told a *Sun* reporter that "business has not been as disastrous as I thought it would be." The park wasn't getting as many casual "drop-in" customers as in past years, but there were plenty of reservations for company and school picnics. Other amusement parks that had been forced to drop Jim Crow had trouble making the transition, with fights sometimes breaking out between white and black teens. That didn't happen during the first years of integration at Gwynn Oak, although James Price noted that some customers didn't want to sit in a roller coaster car with people of another race.

There was a disturbance at the park three years after it integrated, not a black-on-white brawl, but a night of rowdiness on April 24, 1966. A sudden rainstorm caused several hundred teens, mainly African Americans, to swarm out of the park into the parking lot to take a bus home. When there weren't enough buses, the teens began pushing, shoving, and shouting. Some bottles and rocks were thrown at police. It took about seventy police officers—and the arrival of more buses—to restore calm. The next year, there was another troubling event at the park when a 17-year-old boy was killed in a knife attack by a group of teens.

Courtesy Baltimore Sun

At the start of the 1971 summer season, kids rush in for a day of fun in the Kiddie Land section of Gwynn Oak Amusement Park.

Waiting in line for a chance to ride a Ferris wheel at Gwynn Oak Amusement Park during the summer of 1971.

Courtesy Baltimore Sun

These incidents didn't stop hospitals and other organizations from continuing to hold events at the park. Several weeks after the knife attack, a Sunday Bible School Convention that was taking place in Baltimore treated its members' children to a fun afternoon at Gwynn Oak. At the end of that same summer, in August 1967, David Price, one of the park's owners, held a huge party there with free food and rides for about 10,000 people to help his unsuccessful campaign for election to the Baltimore City Council. In September 1969, Baltimore County General Hospital held a party at Gwynn Oak's Dixie Ballroom to raise money for expanding the hospital. A different kind of a fund-raiser occurred there in July 1970, when 13-year-old Bobbie Kemp set a record riding the park's Ferris wheel for fifteen days and nights to help raise money for the Maryland Chapter of the Muscular Dystrophy Association. The following year, a park visitor who had a special way with money was banned from the park because he was too good at one of the games—pitching pennies into a dish—and won too many of the fuzzy toy-bear prizes, which he said he liked to donate to kids in hospitals.

The integration of Gwynn Oak didn't bother René Parent, a longtime fan of the park who lived nearby and was 12 years old in 1963 when it dropped Jim Crow. People warned him that after Gwynn Oak integrated, it might be dangerous, but that didn't stop him and his friends from going to the park as they'd always done. "There were black people there and white people, too. It didn't seem like any big deal, at least to us. We were more interested in how high a score we could get on the pinball machine," he explained. After a few years, though, he felt that he had outgrown Gwynn Oak. He used to love the merry-go-round so much that as a 10-year-old he tried to get extra rides by sneaking onboard without buying a ticket. Another favorite ride of his was the little airplane suspended on a rope that would swoop up and down. But by his mid-teens, he found that "the rides were no longer a thrill," and he stopped going as much.

Some of the people who helped end segregation at the park became regular customers. "I went back to the park with friends as a teenager. It was fun, and convenient. Locally, it was the only place to go," said Lydia Phinney Wilkins, who first went there with her aunt on that undercover mission just before the start of the big July 7, 1963, demonstration. CORE activist Charles Mason also went to Gwynn Oak after it integrated. "I like amusement parks," he said. But fellow CORE volunteer Marie Williams never went back to Gwynn Oak. "They didn't want me there in the first place, so I wasn't interested," she explained. Judge Robert Bell noted, "I'm not big on amusement parks, but my brother and his wife would go and take their kids to Gwynn Oak and I'd go with them." The judge never went back to Hooper's, however, the restaurant where he was arrested as a teen. Mary Sue Welcome stayed away from both Gwynn Oak and Hooper's. "They were a constant reminder of what I was not permitted to do because of the color of my skin," she said.

CHANGING TIMES

A *Sun* reporter wrote a feature story on Gwynn Oak in July 1971, eight years after it integrated, and noted that by then most of the families visiting the park were black. All the kids he saw there that day seemed to be having just as much fun on the merry-go-round, roller coaster, and other rides as he remembered having when he went there as a little boy back when streetcars still brought folks to Gwynn Oak.

Although kids were still having fun on the rides, by 1971, Gwynn Oak was struggling. Some of its buildings were looking rather shabby. The owners had financial problems, which they felt integration had caused. Their money woes could also be blamed on the changing tastes of a society that was now dominated by the automobile. The family car gave people many more options for summertime fun besides going to a nearby, old-time amusement park. Streetcars had stopped rolling past Gwynn Oak in 1955. Some trolley lines survived for a few more years, but the last Baltimore streetcar line went out of service in November 1963, a few months after Gwynn Oak dropped Jim Crow, marking the end of an era.

Attendance was down at other Trolley Parks, too. Big theme parks such as Six Flags were starting to open around the country, providing more exciting thrills and chills than a small, neighborhood park could offer. Hershey Park in nearby Pennsylvania was expanding and adding new rides. Owners of some Trolley Parks called it quits. Glen Echo, the Trolley Park near Washington, D.C., closed in 1968. It had been forced to integrate in 1961 and had experienced racial incidents afterwards, including a wild night of vandalism in 1966 when a huge crowd of teens got out of control. That vandalism may have contributed to the decision by Glen Echo's owners to leave the amusement park business. The closing of Trolley Parks made it harder and more expensive for city folks to enjoy an outing at an amusement park. The big, new theme parks were generally located far outside of cities and charged admission fees. Old-time Trolley Parks usually let customers come in for free, paying only to go on the rides.

In 1971, Gwynn Oak's owners, trying to stay afloat, took out a loan from a bank for half a million dollars, but that apparently wasn't enough to allow the Price brothers to keep the park in top shape. In early June 1972, Baltimore County officials announced that the park could open only if it didn't operate fourteen of its thirty-nine rides. An inspection had found that some rides were unsafe and others had problems that needed to be fixed.

THE BIG STORM

A few weeks later, on June 22, 1972, disaster struck. Hurricane Agnes roared through Baltimore, much earlier in the summer than is usual for these tropical storms. It was the most destructive hurricane ever recorded up until then, causing terrible flooding and damage throughout the Baltimore area. The storm was so devastating that the National Hurricane Center decided never again to use the name Agnes for a hurricane.

Strong winds and heavy rain from Hurricane Agnes swamped Gwynn Oak Amusement Park, ruining many of its buildings and rides. Amazingly, the merry-go-round survived the storm.

Repairing all the damage in the park would have cost about a million dollars, much more than the Price brothers could afford. Gwynn Oak Amusement Park closed for good. The owners declared bankruptcy. The bank that had given them the big loan bought the park, paying much less than the brothers thought the property was worth. "I'm in shock," David Price said at the time of the park's sale. His brother James noted, "That's our life's blood going down the drain."

Although the Price brothers blamed integration for the park's decline, years later, in 2010, Richard B. Price, a son of one of the owners, said, "There were many other reasons the park went down. Integration wasn't the only problem. This was the age of the new super parks. Smaller parks were dying off all over the country. The final straw was Agnes." He felt that ending segregation at the park was "morally the right thing to do." A contractor now, Richard Price was a teenager in 1963, helping to run the park's arcade. He explained that in 1963 "my family thought of the protests as an assault on the business. They wanted to run their business the way they felt was the most efficient. None of the family were racists. It was purely a business move, not racial, even

The land where Gwynn Oak Amusement Park used to be is now a public park.

though it would appear that it was race. Everyone said that was wrong and they adjusted. But it changed the entire way they ran the business."

He noted that the park eventually went from being open seven days a week to being open only on weekends, because, as he explained, many white customers stopped coming and black customers tended to come mainly on Sundays. Just before Hurricane Agnes struck, one of the park's owners told a *Sun* reporter that he hoped the park would be open six days a week that summer. But flood waters from the hurricane put an end to those plans. Richard Price concluded that the story of Gwynn Oak offers a "history lesson. There was a major change [going on] in the country, a change in culture. All facets of the society had this change. Gwynn Oak was just one of the more exposed examples."

Eventually, the land where the park's rides once stood became a picnic and recreation area, owned by Baltimore County. "The buildings are all torn down now. It's just a park," said Lydia Phinney Wilkins. "I live nearby. Every time I drive down that street

I say, 'I helped integrate the park' and feel that I'm part of history." Sharon Langley, also part of the park's history, moved to Atlanta with her mother around the time that Gwynn Oak went out of business, after her parents divorced. Later, during her years as a student at Atlanta's Clark University, she followed in her family's activist tradition and took part in protests against housing discrimination. After college, she worked briefly in film production for directors such as Spike Lee, and then later moved into education, working as a teacher, an instructional coach, an assistant principal, and more recently, a professional-development trainer. "As an adult I've come back to Baltimore and driven by Gwynn Oak," said Ms. Langley. "It was almost impossible to recognize the original park area. Nothing stays the same. Things were bound to change." She's glad her parents had the courage in August 1963 to take her to Gwynn Oak, even though they didn't know what kind of a reception they would face. "Other families might have said 'That's not for us.' My parents had a strong sense of social justice. They knew that change takes people willing to speak up for what's right."

ON THE MALL

Gwynn Oak's lifespan roughly paralleled that of the Jim Crow era. The park opened in the 1890s, as Jim Crow rules were spreading across the South. It closed a few years after the 1964 and 1965 civil rights laws hammered nails into Jim Crow's coffin. Although the park was gone, its merry-go-round lived on to start a new life in a new town.

Having survived Hurricane Agnes, Gwynn Oak's merry-go-round was put up for sale. The buyer, a company that runs concession stands for the Smithsonian, had been looking for a large carousel to replace a small one that had been in front of the Smithsonian for several years. Gwynn Oak's merry-go-round was big enough and beautiful enough to catch the concessionaire's eye.

In 1981, Gwynn Oak's merry-go-round took up residence in Washington. It was installed on the National Mall, directly in

© James Singewald

The Gwynn Oak merry-go-round in its new home on the National Mall, with the Washington Monument in the background.

front of the Smithsonian's Arts and Industries Building. Renamed the Carousel on the Mall, the ride was the same as at Gwynn Oak, although it had received a fresh coat of paint. In 1996, a sea dragon joined the ride, a special treat to mark the 150th anniversary of the Smithsonian. A spinning-tub car also came aboard, a replica of one the Allan Herschell company made. Another change: After a few years the ride's pipe organ was replaced by a CD player.

The horses, however, have remained the same. When kids climb into the saddles, they can look down the Mall and see the Washington Monument. Just beyond that is the Lincoln Memorial, where Rev. Dr. Martin Luther King, Jr., stood on August 28, 1963, describing his dream of a just and peaceful world. He never saw this freedom-go-round of a ride take its place on the Mall, struck down as he was in 1968 by a killer filled with hate. But Dr. King's words live on. This merry-go-round provides an example of his dream brought to life, as big kids, little kids, young kids, old kids—kids of all races and religions—circle round and round, up and down, having fun together.

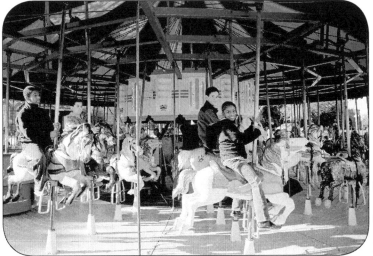

© James Singewald

Riding the Gwynn Oak merry-go-round in its new location in front of the Smithsonian are (left to right) Cameron Carney, Elijah and Daniel Conry, and Jhade Carney. Jhade and Cameron's great aunt is civil rights pioneer Sarah Keys Evans. (See page 93.)

Follow-Up

B EING ARRESTED AT GWYNN OAK "was one of the key moments in my life," said Arthur Waskow, a rabbi who founded the Shalom Center, dedicated to world peace and fighting discrimination. Still on display in his office is the photo of his Gwynn Oak arrest, which changed him from just studying protests to taking part in them. Many Gwynn Oak protest veterans (including those listed below) continued to be active supporters of civil rights and other causes:

- Rev. Marion C. Bascom was a leader in helping to restore calm in Baltimore in 1968 during the disturbances after the assassination of Dr. King. Rev. Bascom retired in 1995 after forty-six years as pastor of Douglas Memorial Community Church, but has remained active in community affairs.
- Alison Turaj Brown was arrested many more times in civil rights demonstrations. She lived for many years in New Jersey, working in anti-poverty and Head Start programs and helping to uncover Medicare fraud.
- Lew Buckler became a minister and then an electrical engineer who worked for the government.
- Walter Carter served with several Baltimore groups that offered job training or help with housing issues, until his death in 1971.
- Ed Chance continued, until his death in 2003, to be a social worker at a Baltimore psychiatric hospital, the first black to run a clinical department there.
- The Colemans: Lu Coleman became a Baltimore schoolteacher and, after retiring, tutored in an after-school program for inner-city kids. After she and James Coleman divorced, he was a professor at the University of Chicago until his death in 1995. Their son Tom is a retired investment banker; John works on environmental issues with Native Americans in Wisconsin; Steve does education research in Washington.

- Mike Furstenberg served in the Peace Corps in Brazil and then became an educational psychologist in Massachusetts.
- Linda Grant is a public affairs officer for the Washington, D.C., Department of Public Works. Her mother, Mabel Grant Young, retired from teaching and kept living in Baltimore.
- The Langleys: Charles C. Langley, Jr., continued at Social Security until his death in the late 1970s. Marian Langley, who died in 2003, earned a master's in public health from Johns Hopkins, worked in the Maternal and Child Health program of the federal government in Georgia, and after retiring, started a gallery for African American artists. Sharon Langley, after graduating from Atlanta's Clark University, worked in film production and then moved into education, earning a master's degree and working as a teacher, assistant principal, instructional coach, and more recently as a professional-development facilitator and trainer.
- Margaret Levi is a professor of political science at the University of Washington and also at the U.S. Studies Centre of the University of Sydney in Australia.

© James Singewald

Steve Coleman, a baby when his parents were arrested at Gwynn Oak in July 1963, brought his daughter Lilah to Washington in 2010 to ride the old Gwynn Oak merry-go-round.

- Charles Mason was a parole officer who served in a program to help at-risk youngsters and now recruits retirees for volunteer work through a Baltimore city program.
- The Mitchells: Juanita Jackson Mitchell kept doing what she had been doing until her death in 1992. In her 70s, she launched a "Stop the Killing Campaign" to protest killings within the black community. Her husband, Clarence Mitchell, Jr., continued as the NAACP's chief lobbyist in Washington until his death in 1984. Her sons Michael and Clarence, III, became lawyers; Keiffer became a doctor; her youngest son, George, became a real estate developer.
- Robert Moore became the head of Maryland's health care workers' union, 1199E-DC.
- John Roemer is a Baltimore private school teacher and librarian, specializing in a course on civil rights; he served for several years as executive director of Maryland's chapter of the American Civil Liberties Union.
- Judge Robert Watts, who died in 1998, was a judge in Baltimore from 1963 until 1985, when he joined a Baltimore law firm. His son Rodney Binx Watts was a lawyer in California for thirty years and returned to Baltimore in the 1990s to become a professional golfer, teaching golf to young people.
- Mary Sue Welcome became a lawyer and by 2010 was a Maryland assistant attorney general, working on health care issues. Her mother, State Senator Verda Welcome, continued to serve in political office until she retired in 1982, eight years before her death in 1990.
- Lydia Phinney Wilkins is a program analyst in the Office of Employment Opportunity and Civil Rights.
- Marie Williams worked at Greater Baltimore Medical Center as a unit clerk and also in Medical Records, earning "employee of the month" awards. Her sister, Carolyn Stith, was a community organizer and director of a neighborhood service center in East Baltimore until her death in 1981.

Timeline

1894	Gwynn Oak Amusement Park opens
1896	*Plessy v. Ferguson* Supreme Court decision
1930	Gandhi's Salt March protest in India
1931	City-Wide Young People's Forum founded in Baltimore
1933	Don't Buy Where You Can't Work boycott in Baltimore
1935	Lillie May Carroll Jackson heads Baltimore's NAACP
1936	University of Maryland Law School integrates
	Arthur B. Price, Sr., begins leasing Gwynn Oak Amusement Park
1942	March on Annapolis
	CORE is founded in Chicago
1946	*Morgan v. Virginia* Supreme Court decision
1947	New merry-go-round arrives at Gwynn Oak
	Jackie Robinson joins Brooklyn Dodgers
	CORE's Journey of Reconciliation bus campaign
	Gandhi's protest movement wins India its independence from Britain
1948	End of racial segregation in U.S. military
	Interracial tennis tournament protest in Baltimore
	Gandhi assassinated in India
1952	Poly, Baltimore's science-and-math high school, integrates
	Baltimore's Ford's Theatre ends segregated seating
1953	Baltimore's CORE chapter founded
1953–55	Lunch counter sit-ins in Baltimore

1954	Marian Anderson performs at Lyric Theatre
	Brown v. Board of Education decision
	Baltimore public schools end segregation
1955	Lunch counters at Read's integrate
	CIG founded—Civic Interest Group
	CORE's first demonstration at Gwynn Oak
	Montgomery Bus Boycott begins
1959	Five protestors arrested at Gwynn Oak
1960	Lunch-counter sit-ins throughout the South
	CIG protests at department store restaurants
1960–63	CIG and CORE restaurant sit-ins: Baltimore, Route 40, and elsewhere in Maryland
1961	CORE's Freedom Rides down South
1962	Baltimore Public Accommodations Law
1962	Embassies boycott All Nations Day Festival
	Parochial schools begin boycott of Gwynn Oak
1963	CIG succeeds in integrating Northwood Theatre
	Mass arrests in Birmingham, Alabama
	Maryland Public Accommodations Law
	July 4 and 7 demonstrations at Gwynn Oak
	Gwynn Oak drops Jim Crow rules on August 28
	August 28 March on Washington for Jobs and Freedom
	President John F. Kennedy assassinated
1964	Broader Public Accommodations Law in Maryland
	U.S. Congress passes the 1964 Civil Rights Act
1965	U.S. Congress passes the 1965 Voting Rights Act
1968	Rev. Dr. Martin Luther King, Jr., assassinated
1972	Hurricane Agnes forces Gwynn Oak to close
1981	Gwynn Oak merry-go-round moves to the National Mall in Washington, D.C.

Notes

Listed below are sources, identified in most cases by the last name of the author, for quoted material, with the first and last words of each quote given. For people interviewed by the author (see bibliography), nearly all their quotes come from the interviews. For the few instances in which quotes from them come from another source, it is noted here.

All quotes from Juanita Jackson Mitchell, Robert Watts, Verda Welcome, and Walter Sondheim, Jr., come from the oral histories they recorded for the Maryland Historical Society and so are not included in the following listing.

ABBREVIATIONS

Brown	Text of *Brown v. Board of Education*
JJM	Juanita Jackson Mitchell
HT	*New York Herald Tribune*
JFK-R	Kennedy, John F. "Radio and Television Report to the American People on Civil Rights"
JFK-S	Kennedy, John F. "Statement by the President on the March on Washington for Jobs and Freedom"
King-A	*Autobiography of Martin Luther King, Jr.*
King-Hope	King, Martin Luther, Jr. *A Testament of Hope*
Meier-C	Meier, August and Elliott Rudwick. *CORE*
Meier-W	Meier, August. *A White Scholar and the Black Community*
NYT	*New York Times*
OH-MD	Oral history—Maryland Historical Society
OH-UB	Oral history—University of Baltimore
Waskow-R	Waskow, Arthur I. *Running Riot*
WP	*Washington Post*

CHAPTER 1

Pages

2 "Gwynn Oak stood . . . challenged": *The Sun*, Aug. 22, 1963.

9 "When you . . . to wait": King-Hope, pp. 292–3.

12 "We have . . . Americans": Bascom, OH-UB.

CHAPTER 2

Pages

33   "God opened . . . it": JJM, OH-MD July 25, 1975.
36   "Mr. McKeldin . . . community": Bascom, OH-MD.
37   "We must . . . separate": *The Sun*, May 22, 1944.

CHAPTER 3

Pages

42   "These discriminatory . . . is unjust": *Afro-American*, May 30, 1953.
44   "I had learned . . . home": Tygiel.
46   "We . . . to listen": Meier-C, p. 10.
50   "We just . . . happens": *The Sun*, Feb. 8, 2011.
56   "the policy . . . and minds": Brown.
63   "As good . . . we do": *Afro-American*, May 18, 1954.
63   "establishments . . . public": *The Sun*, Mar. 16, 1955.

CHAPTER 4

Pages

64   "We have . . . peoples": *Afro-American*, Sept. 1, 1962.
67   "We have to . . . pioneers": *Afro-American*, Aug. 20, 1955.
69   "first step": *The Sun*, Sept. 2, 1957.
69   "This is an . . . negotiate": *The Sun*, Sept. 2, 1957.
71   "Get . . . rope": *NYT*, Sept. 7, 1959.
71   "I am amazed . . . unpunished": *The Sun*, Sept. 24, 1959.
73   "economic suicide": *The Sun*, Sept. 5, 1960.
73   "We are not . . . wrong": *The Sun*, Sept. 5, 1960.
74   "My mother . . . segregation": Levi (oral history).

CHAPTER 5

Pages

78   "We will match . . . laws": King-Hope, p. 485.
83   "We will so . . . process": King-Hope, p. 485.
84   "depends . . . support": Gandhi, p. 145.
84   "No longer did . . . King": Farmer, p. 186.
91   "We must . . . segregation": *Afro-American*, July 18, 1961.
92   "We had been . . . freeze": Barnes, p. 165.
93   "when the heat . . . Rides": Barnes, p. 187.

CHAPTER 6

Pages

94 "I shall ... beings": *Afro-American*, July 16, 1960.

104 "Every time I ... shudder": *Afro-American*, July 16, 1960.

105 "We are trying ... did": *Afro-American*, July 16, 1960.

107 "To those who ... violence": *The Sun*, July 16, 1961.

107 "sit-in ... Americans": *Afro-American*, July 18, 1961.

107 "It would have ... action": *The Sun*, July 16, 1961.

CHAPTER 7

Pages

116 "These students ... end": *Afro-American*, Feb. 23, 1963.

120-1 "We have no ... out": *Afro-American*, Feb. 23, 1963.

121 "continue ... crises": Barnes, p. 187.

124 "I am ... reputation": *The Sun*, Feb. 22, 1963.

125 "management ... Baltimore": Meier-W, p. 143.

CHAPTER 8

Pages

128 "like a ... organized": Dilts, *The Sun*, Dec. 1, 1968.

130 "I belong ... race": WP, July 1, 1960.

131 "white man's party": *The Sun*, Sept. 3, 1962.

132 "knowingly ... act": WP, Sept. 6, 1962.

133 "the backbone ... business": *The Sun*, June 25, 1964.

133 "the public ... business": *The Sun*, Aug. 31, 1962.

136 "Changes in ... government": *The Sun*, May 7, 1960.

137 "When the law ... right": *The Sun*, March 9, 1963.

137-8 "Equality ... people": *The Sun*, March 9, 1963.

138 "There is no ... discrimination": *Afro-American*, March 19, 1963.

CHAPTER 9

Pages

140 "One hundred ... free": JFK-R.

141 "This was ... opened": *Afro-American*, Dec. 18, 1962.

144 "give all ... public." JFK-R.

147 "What we ... effective": King-Hope, p. 344.

147 "The civil ... Lincoln": Nunnelly, p. 164.

147   "demonstrations . . . action": *NYT*, June 22, 1963.

147   "all-out effort": *NYT*, June 19, 1963.

149   "Nonviolent . . . expensive": *The Sun*, June 18, 1963.

151   "leave us . . . with us": *Afro-American*, June 29, 1963.

151–2   "We have . . . tactics": *Afro-American*, July 2, 1963.

153   "Chief Lally . . . park": *Afro-American*, July 2, 1963.

153   "The time . . . come": Bascom, OH-MD.

CHAPTER 10

Pages

154   "any individual . . . law": King-Hope, p. 294.

155   "The churches . . . themselves": *NYT*, July 5, 1963.

156   "been . . . demonstrations": *The Sun*, July 5, 1963.

157   "I am the . . . preached": *The Sun*, July 5, 1963.

157   "We live . . . them in": *The Sun*, July 5, 1963.

159   "I don't know . . . community": *The Sun*, July 5, 1963.

160   "I think . . . July": *The Sun*, July 5, 1963.

160   "We had . . . police": *The Sun*, July 5, 1963.

167   "the first . . . discrimination": *NYT*, July 5, 1963.

CHAPTER 11

Pages

172   "parishes . . . demonstration": *The Sun*, July 8, 1963.

172   "Go down . . . go": *Afro-American*, July 9, 1963.

175   "are not . . . park": *NYT*, July 8, 1963.

176   "This is . . . off": *The Sun*, July 8, 1963.

177   "Hey, you . . . here": *Afro-American*, July 9, 1963.

177   "I have seen . . . hate": *Afro-American*, July 9, 1963.

178   "I felt . . . hatred": Waskow-R, p. 5.

180   "upholding . . . land": *Afro-American*, July 9, 1963.

181   "There comes a . . . jailbird": *Afro-American*, July 9, 1963.

185   "I had to . . . in": *Afro-American*, July 9, 1963.

CHAPTER 12

Pages

186   "We reluctantly . . . democracy": *HT*, July 6, 1963.

187   "wasting . . . self-hypnosis": *Afro-American*, July 9, 1963.

188 "There is an . . . Maryland": *Afro-American*, July 9, 1963.

188–9 "I don't . . . degree": *The Sun*, July 10, 1963.

189 "if we can . . . progress": *The Sun*, July 10, 1963.

190 "We're . . . feet": *The Sun*, July 12, 1963.

190 "Morally . . . integrated": *The Sun*, July 10, 1963.

190 "flagrant abuse": *The Sun*, July 10, 1963.

191 "an . . . party": *The Sun*, July 16, 1963.

191 "We have . . . negotiations": *The Sun*, July 16, 1963.

193 "disgusting": *The Sun*, July 10, 1963.

193 "repulsive": *The Sun*, July 7, 1963.

193 "life itself": *The Sun*, July 19, 1963.

193 "their . . . law": *The Sun*, July 20, 1963.

193 "It is . . . Party": *The Sun*, July 13, 1963.

193 "prejudices . . . strife": *The Sun*, July 19, 1963.

194 "The longer . . . control": *The Sun*, July 19, 1963.

194 "possible bloodshed": *The Sun*, July 20, 1963.

194 "We are . . . holocaust": *The Sun*, July 20, 1963.

194 "You all . . . understand": *The Sun*, July 20, 1963.

195 "Money is . . . game": Bascom, OH-MD.

197 "a good . . . the state": *NYT*, July 21, 1963.

197 "depressing . . . sky": King-Hope, p. 293.

CHAPTER 13

Pages

200 "I hope . . . park": *The Sun*, Aug. 29, 1963.

201 "My first . . . reporters": *The Sun*, Aug. 29, 1963.

203–4 "I don't . . . value": *The Sun*, Aug. 29, 1963.

205 "I hope . . . came": *The Sun*, Aug. 29, 1963.

205 "I am very . . . came": *Afro-American*, Aug. 31, 1963.

206 "to give . . . deserve": *The Sun*, Aug. 28, 1963.

209 "We have . . . here today": JFK-S.

CHAPTER 14

Pages

214 "Courage . . . of fear": Farmer, p. 3.

215 "There has . . . bright": *The Sun*, Sept. 13, 1963.

216 "business has . . . would be": *The Sun*, June 25, 1964.

220 "I'm in . . . drain": *The Sun*, June 26, 1974.

Bibliography
and Sources

INTERVIEWS WITH AUTHOR

By Telephone

Jim Abbate, March 2010
Robert Bell, Feb. 17, 2010
Alison Turaj Brown, Feb. 4, 2010
Lewis M. Buckler, Feb. 29, 2010
Lucille Coleman, May 27, 2009
Tom, John and Steve Coleman, June 1, 2009
Joyce I. Dennison, Jan. 29, 2010
Lois B. Feinblatt, Dec. 8, 2010
Michael Furstenberg, March 7, 2010
Linda Grant, July 2009
Stan Hunter, Aug./Sept. 2010
Sharon Langley, July 2009, Aug. 26, 2010
Margaret and Beatty Levi, Sept. 5, 1010
Charles Mason, Feb. 21 and March 15, 2010
Dr. Keiffer Mitchell, Sr., Oct. 5, 2010
Michael Mitchell, Sr., Oct. 5, 2010
René Parent, March 1, 2011
Richard B. Price, Nov. 26, 2010
John Roemer, March 12, 2010
Rudy Toth, March 13, 2011
Arthur Waskow, Feb. 4, 2010
Rodney Binx Watts, Jan. 7, 2011
Mary Sue Welcome, Feb. 18, 2010
Lydia Phinney Wilkins, July 29, 2009
Marie Williams, Feb. 8, 2010
Mabel Grant Young, July 16, 2009

By E-mail

Billie Garner Brown, January 2011
Carol Buckler, June 20, 2010
Jean Hess, April 2009
Patrick Wentzel, May 13, 2009

BOOKS

Arsenault, Raymond. *Freedom Riders: 1961 and the Struggle for Racial Justice.* New York: Oxford Univ. Press, 2006.

Barnes, Catherine A. *Journey from Jim Crow: The Desegregation of Southern Transit.* New York: Columbia Univ. Press, 1983.

Baum, Howell S. *Brown in Baltimore: School Desegregation and the Limits of Liberalism.* Ithaca: Cornell Univ. Press, 2010.

Branch, Taylor. *Parting the Waters: America in the King Years 1954–63.* New York: Simon and Schuster, 1988.

———. *Pillar of Fire: America in the King Years 1963–65.* New York: Simon and Schuster, 1998.

Brugger, Robert J. *Maryland, A Middle Temperament: 1634–1980.* Baltimore: Johns Hopkins Univ. Press, 1996.

Durr, Kenneth D. *Behind the Backlash: White Working-Class Politics in Baltimore, 1940–1980.* Chapel Hill: Univ. of North Carolina Press, 2007.

Farmer, James. *Lay Bare the Heart: An Autobiography of the Civil Rights Movement.* New York: Arbor House, 1985.

Fried, Frederick. *A Pictorial History of the Carousel.* New York: A.S. Barnes and Co., 1964.

Gandhi, Mahatma. *The Essential Gandhi: An Anthology of His Writings on His Life, Work, and Ideas.* Ed. Louis Fischer. New York: Vintage Books, 2002.

Gitlin, Todd. *The Sixties: Years of Hope Days of Rage.* New York: Bantam Books, 1987.

Harwood, Herbert H., Jr. *Baltimore Streetcars: The Postwar Years.* Baltimore: Johns Hopkins Univ. Press, 2003.

Kenny, Katherine, and Eleanor Randrup. *Juanita Jackson Mitchell: Freedom Fighter.* Baltimore: Publish America, 2005.

King, Martin Luther, Jr. *A Testament of Hope: The Essential Writings and Speeches of Martin Luther King, Jr.* Ed. James Melvin Washington. New York: Harper One, 1986.

———. *The Autobiography of Martin Luther King, Jr.* Ed. Clayborne Carson. New York: Warner Books, 1998.

———. *Why We Can't Wait.* New York: Signet Classics, 2000.

Manns, William. *Painted Ponies: American Carousel Art.* Santa Fe, NM: Zon International Publishing, 1986.

Mayer, Robert H. *When the Children Marched: The Birmingham Civil Rights Movement.* Berkeley Heights, NJ: Enslow Publishers, 2008.

McWhorter, Diane. *Carry Me Home: Birmingham, Alabama.* New York: Simon & Schuster, 2001.

McWhorter, Diane. *A Dream of Freedom: The Civil Rights Movement from 1954 to 1968.* New York: Scholastic, 2004.

Meier, August. *A White Scholar and the Black Community, 1945–1965: Essays and Reflections.* Amherst: Univ. of Massachusetts Press, 1992.

Meier, August, and Elliott Rudwick. *CORE: A Study in the Civil Rights Movement 1942–1968.* Urbana, IL: Univ. of Illinois Press, 1973.

Mills, Barbara. *"Got My Mind Set On Freedom": Maryland's Story of Black & White Activism 1663–2000.* Westminster, MD: Heritage Books, 2007.

Nathan, Amy. *Take a Seat—Make a Stand: A Hero in the Family.* New York: iUniverse, 2006.

Newfield, Jack. *Somebody's Gotta Tell It: The Upbeat Memoir of a Working-Class Journalist.* New York: St. Martin's Press, 2001.

Nunnelly, William A. *Bull Connor.* Tuscaloosa: Univ. of Alabama Press, 1991.

Orser, W. Edward. *Blockbusting in Baltimore: The Edmondson Village Story.* Lexington: Univ. Press of Kentucky, 1994.

Orser, W. Edward. *The Gwynns Falls: Baltimore Greenway to the Chesapeake Bay.* Charleston, SC: The History Press, 2008.

Pastan, Amy. *Gandhi: A Photographic Story of a Life.* New York: DK Publishing, 2006.

Pietila, Antero. *Not in My Neighborhood: How Bigotry Shaped a Great American City.* Chicago: Ivan R. Dee, 2010.

Rhodes, Jason. *Maryland's Amusement Parks.* Chicago: Arcadia Publishing, 2005.

Rice, T. D. *Jim Crow, American: Selected Songs and Plays.* Ed. W. T. Lhamon, Jr. Cambridge: Harvard Univ. Press, 2003.

Schechter, Danny. *The More You Watch, The Less You Know.* New York: Seven Stories Press, 1997.

Sidney Hollander Foundation. *Toward Equality: Baltimore's Progress Report.* Baltimore: Maryland Historical Society, 2003.

Smith, C. Fraser. *Here Lies Jim Crow: Civil Rights in Maryland.* Baltimore: Johns Hopkins Univ. Press, 2008.

Southern, Eileen. *Music of Black Americans: A History.* New York: W. W. Norton, 1997.

Stanton, Mary. *Freedom Walk.* Jackson: Univ. Press of Mississippi, 2003.

Waskow, Arthur I. *From Race Riot to Sit-In, 1919 and the 1960s: A Study in the Connections Between Conflict and Violence.* New York: Doubleday, 1966.

———. *Running Riot: A Journey Through the Official Disasters and Creative Disorder in American Society.* New York: Herder and Herder, 1970.

Watson, Denton L. *Lion in the Lobby: Clarence Mitchell, Jr.'s Struggle for the Passage of Civil Rights Laws.* New York: William Morrow, 1990.

Woodward, C. Vann. *The Strange Career of Jim Crow.* New York: Oxford Univ. Press, 2002.

MAGAZINE ARTICLES

Backs, Jean. "For Your Amusement." *Ohio State Parks Magazine*, Spring/ Summer 2000.

Charles, Barbara. "Merry-Go-Rounds." *Smithsonian*, July 1972.

Kershner, Jim. "Segregation in Spokane." *Columbia Magazine*, vol. 14, no. 4, Winter 2000-01.

"March on Gwynn Oak Park." *Time Magazine*, July 12, 1963.

Mendelsohn, Ink. "Around and Around on the Carry-us-all." *The Torch: A Monthly Newspaper for the Smithsonian Institution*, April 1981.

Milobsky, David. "Power from the Pulpit: Baltimore's African-American Clergy, 1950-1970." *Maryland Historical Magazine*, vol. 89, no. 3, 1994.

Palumbos, Robert. "Student Involvement in the Baltimore Civil Rights Movement 1953-63." *Maryland Historical Magazine*, vol. 94, Winter 1999.

Shoemaker, Sandy M. "'We Shall Overcome, Someday': The Equal Rights Movement in Baltimore 1935-1942." *Maryland Historical Magazine*, vol. 89, Fall 1994.

"Time Magazine Person of the Year: Martin Luther King, Jr." *Time Magazine*, Jan. 3, 1964.

Tygiel, Jules. "The Court-Martial of Jackie Robinson." *American Heritage Magazine*, vol. 35, issue 5, Aug./Sept. 1984.

Vernon, John, "Jim Crow, Meet Lieutenant Robinson: A 1944 Court-Martial." *Prologue Magazine*, vol. 40, no. 1, Spring 2008.

Wexler, Laura. "The Last Dance." *Style: Smart Living in Baltimore*, vol. 11, no. 5, Sept./Oct. 2003.

Wolcott, Victoria W. "Recreation and Race in the Postwar City: Buffalo's 1956 Crystal Beach Riot." *Journal of American History*, June 2006.

———. "Integrated Leisure in Segregated Cities: Amusement Parks and Racial Conflict in the Post-War North." Unpublished paper, presented at the Urban History Associates, Oct. 2004, available online at: http://hdl.handle.net/1802/2931.

NEWSPAPER ARTICLES

Feature Articles and Op-Ed Pieces

Benjamin, Philip. "Aroused College Students Enlist in Negroes' Cause," *The New York Times*, July 7, 1963.

Branch, Taylor. "Dr. King's Newest Marcher," *The New York Times*, Sept. 4, 2010.

Dilts, James D. "The Warning Trumpet: CORE Is 'The Only Voice Black People Ever Had,'" *The Sun*, Dec. 1, 1968.

Jones, Edgar L. "Maryland School Integration," *The Sun*, May 5, 1957.

Jones, Melissa. "Druid Hill Park Turns 150," *The Afro*, September 15, 2010.

Kaufman, A. Robert. "Integrating Ford's," *The Sun*, Sept. 17, 1993.

Langley, Sharon. "Why I Marched on Forsyth County," *The Atlanta Voice*, vol. 21, no. 24, Feb. 7–13, 1987.

Moores, Lew. "Coney Island Segregation Ended 40 Years Ago," *The Cincinnati Enquirer*, May 27, 2001.

O'Brien, Dennis. "The Castle of One's Skin: Blacks Recall Protest They Staged in 1960 in City Restaurant," *The Sun*, Nov. 13, 1994.

Rehert, Isaac. "Gwynn Oak Park Stirs Thoughts of Childhood," *The Sun*, July 15, 1971.

———. "Amusement Park Remains Thrill-Seekers Paradise," *The Sun*, July 17, 1971.

Samuels, Gertrude. "School Desegregation: A Case History," *The New York Times*, May 8, 1955.

———. "Even More Crucial Than in the South," *The New York Times*, June 30, 1963.

Schoettler, Carl. "Tennis Everyone?" *The Sun*, April 24, 2003.

Siegel, Eric. "A Nonpolitical Mitchell, Who Is a Doctor and an Artist," *The Sun*, Feb. 5, 1984.

Smith, Linell. "Justice at Gwynn Oak," *The Sun*, Aug. 23, 1998.

———. "Touched by the Spirit," *The Sun*, Aug. 24, 1998.

"Song of Freedom," *Jewish Times*, April 28, 2006.

Venutolo, Anthony. "Leisure Activities Remained Quietly Segregated Even As Northern New Jersey's Public Spaces Were Integrated," *The Star-Ledger*, Feb. 26, 2009.

Wallace, Weldon. "The City We Live In," *The Sun*, March 14–17, 1955.

Welcome, Mary Sue. "Three Hours Behind the Bars," *Baltimore Afro-American*, July 16, 1960

Williams, James D. "Afro Editor Tells of Jailing," *Baltimore Afro-American*, July 9, 1963

News Stories in Newspapers and Magazines

ON GWYNN OAK AMUSEMENT PARK. *Baltimore Afro-American*—1955: Aug. 20, Nov. 19; 1956: Sept. 4, 8; 1957: Aug. 31; 1959: Sept. 8, Dec. 15; 1960: April 19; 1962:Aug. 28, Sept. 1, 8, 11, 18; 1963: March 19, May 21, 28, June 29, July 2, 6, 9, 16, 23, Aug. 28, 31, Sept.1, 24, Nov. 12, Dec. 21; 1967: July 15; 1971: June 12. *Billboard*—1942: May 16, Oct. 10; 1943: Dec 4; 1944: Dec 30; 1945: Jan 6; 1952: April 19; 1953: April 25; 1955: May 21; 1956: March 3; 1957: July 8, Dec 16; 1963: July 27. *New York Herald Tribune*—1963: July 6, 8, 12, 14. *The New York Times*—1959: Sept. 7; 1963: June 30, July 5, 8, 20, 21, Sept. 1. *The Sun*—1909: May 9, June 30, July 18; 1954: Aug. 30; 1955: Sept. 4, 5; 1957: Sept. 2;

1958: Sept. 1; 1959: Sept. 6, 7, 24; 1960: April 9, 19, May 7, Sept. 5; 1961: Jan. 19, 21, Aug. 31, Sept. 4; 1962: Aug. 25, 26, 29-31, Sept. 2, 3, 9, 10; 1963: March 9, May 19, 21, 31, June 2, 5, 18, July 5-21, Aug. 18, 22, 28, 29, Sep. 2, 13; 1964: June 25, July 7, Oct. 8; 1965: March 10, June 2; 1966: April 25, Aug. 8; 1967: May 16, June 25, Aug. 30; 1969: Sept. 12; 1970: June 16, July 5; 1971: June 8; 1972: June 1, 3; 1974: June 4, 26; 1979: Jan. 9; 1980: March 12; 1991: Nov. 20; 1997: June 22. *The Washington Post*—1959: Sept. 7; 1963: July 7, Sept. 14; 1962: Aug. 26, Sept. 4, 6, 11.

ON OTHER CIVIL RIGHTS EVENTS. *Baltimore Afro-American*—1953: May 30; 1954: May 18; 1955: Nov. 19; 1956: Feb. 7; 1957: Jan. 1, 19, June 14; 1958: July 1, 19, Aug. 23, Sept. 27; 1960: July 16; 1961: July 18; 1962: June 12, Aug. 14, 18, Dec. 18; 1963: Jan 8, Feb. 23, March 19, April 9, Aug.10. *The New York Times*—1930: April 3-6; 1954: Sep. 21, Oct. 6, 8, 31; 1955: May 8, Sept. 24; 1959: Jan. 4, 20, Feb. 4; 1961: Nov. 6; 1963: June 19, 22, 30, July 4, 7, Sept. 12. *The Sun*—1944: May 22; 1948: July 12; 1953: May 29, Sept. 17, 24, Nov. 14, 27, Dec. 14, 29; 1954: Jan. 8, Oct. 1, 2, 5, 8; 1955: Sept. 4; 1960: Feb. 23, April 1; 1961: July 16, 19, Nov. 15, 18, 30, Dec. 2, 17; 1962: Jan 14, 18, Feb. 6, 7, 12, March 11, May 2, 10, 13, June 2, 5, 10, 11, July 10, Aug. 29, 30; 1963: Feb. 22, 23, March 12, 13, March 30, May 1, 6, 13, 21, Aug. 7, 26,28, 29, Sept. 14; 1964: Oct.8; 2010: Mar. 27; 2011: Feb. 8 *The Washington Post*—1960: July 1, 10, Aug. 21, 25, Sept. 8, 12, Nov. 3; 1961: March 15, April 1, July 25; 1966: April 12, 22, May 5; 1967: March 21; 1968: May 2; 1969: April 2; 2000: July 30.

ON ARTHUR PRICE, SR. *Baltimore Afro-American*—1954: May 18; 1955: Jan. 29, Feb. 5, 26. *Billboard*—1944: Dec. 30; 1957: Dec. 16. *The Sun*—1951: May 15; 1954: April 17, May 19, June 2, July 11, Aug. 16; 1955: Feb. 10, March 2; 1974: June 4; 1991: Nov. 19.

Editorials and Letters to the Editor

Baltimore Afro-American—1955: Nov. 19; 1962: Sept. 1; 1963: Feb. 23. *The Sun*—1947: June 12; 1959: Sept. 24; 1961: Jan. 21; 1962: May 10; 1963: July 6, 7, 10, 13, 17–20, Aug. 22. *The New York Times*—1963: July 8.

INTERNET SOURCES

Brown v. Board of Education, 347 U.S. 483 (1954)—http://www.nationalcenter. org/brown.html.

"The Civil Rights Movement in Virginia: Massive Resistance"—http:// www.vahistorical.org/civilrights/massiveresistance.htm.

Kennedy, John F. "Radio and Television Report to the American People on Civil Rights" June 11, 1963—http://www.presidency.ucsb.edu/ws/index. php?pid=9271.

Kennedy, John F. "Statement by the President on the March on Washington for Jobs and Freedom." Aug. 28, 1963—http://www.presidency.ucsb.edu/ws/index.php?pid=9383#axzz1LPc4zrm8.

"Martin Luther King, Jr., and the Global Freedom Struggle"—http://mlk-kpp01.stanford.edu/index.php/encyclopedia/encyclopedia/enc_national_council_of_the_churches_of_christ_in_america_ncc/.

Rudolph, Lewis. "Forty Years of Determined Struggle: A Political Portrait of Robert Moore, a Baltimore Leader"—http://www.nathanielturner.com/fortyyearsofdeterminedstrugg.htm.

"The St. Louis Story, the Integration of a Public School System"—http://www.eric.ed.gov:80/ERICWebPortal/search/detailmini.jsp?_nfpb=true&_&ERICExtSearch_SearchValue_0=ED001929&ERICExtSearch_SearchType_0=no&accno=ED001929.

ORAL HISTORIES

Bascom, Marion C. (interviewed June 18, 1976), Juanita Jackson Mitchell (interviewed July 15, 1975; July 25, 1975; January 10, 1976), Virginia Mitchell Kiah (interviewed July 25, 1975; January 10, 1976), Walter Sondheim, Jr. (interviewed October 19, 1971; September 27, 1976), Robert Watts (interviewed February 2, 1976), Verda Welcome (interviewed July 8. 1976). Transcripts are available from the Maryland Historical Society, which recorded the interviews.

Bascom, Marion C., transcripts of interviews recorded in 2006 by the University of Baltimore as part of "Baltimore 68: Riots and Rebirth" are available online at: http://archives.ubalt.edu/bsr/oral-histories/oral-histories1.html.

Levi, Margaret, interview recorded on November 21, 2000, for the WTO History Project of the University of Washington. Transcript available at: http://depts.washington.edu/wtohist/interviews/Levi.pdf.

OTHER

"You Don't Have to Ride Jim Crow!" DVD about CORE's Journey of Reconciliation is available from www.robinwashington.com.

Goldstein, Ruth. "The Racial Segregation of Three Private Schools: A Case Study of the Park School of Baltimore, Gilman School and St. Paul's School for Girls." High school research paper, 1996.

Author's Note

I grew up in Baltimore in the 1950s and 1960s. Until recently, I never knew that on August 28, 1963, the day of the March on Washington, not far from the house where I lived as a child, another event occurred that was also a civil rights milestone. I learned about this in 2008 from a book my brother recommended, *Here Lies Jim Crow* by C. Fraser Smith. I had just finished writing *Take a Seat—Make a Stand*, a book about civil rights hero Sarah Keys Evans, who did what Rosa Parks did three years earlier than Mrs. Parks. My brother thought I'd be interested in the Smith book because it too reported on events overlooked by standard histories. I was intrigued by its brief mention of the role played by a little girl in Baltimore on August 28, 1963. I set out to learn how that event came to happen.

In 1963, Baltimore was a city of ethnically and religiously separate neighborhoods. I grew up in Hunting Ridge, a largely white Protestant neighborhood on the western edge of town, but was lucky to break out of the stranglehold of separate neighborhoods by going to Western High School, an all-girls public high school that draws students from across the city. Our class entered Western a few years after *Brown v. Board of Education* integrated Baltimore schools. We felt we were part of a new era in which people of all races and religions would learn finally to get along.

Even though I became friends with girls from different backgrounds than mine and began to be a peripheral part of a group that was active politically, I was aware of only a small sliver of the civil rights events of those days. In the past three years, I've been filling in the gaps. An excellent two-part series by Linell Smith from 1998 in the *Sun* helped get my research going. I began reading back issues of newspapers along with books, articles, and also transcripts of oral histories of local activists recorded by the Maryland Historical Society. Using the Internet, I tracked down other activists and am grateful that so many kindly agreed to be interviewed.

I've always regretted that in August 1963 I didn't join my new Western High School friends and go to the March on Washington. Instead, I knuckled under to my parents' fears that violence might break out. I've always been annoyed with them for that—and with myself, too.

My parents were firm believers in equal rights for all and had no problem with my volunteering that summer with a civil rights group called the Northern Student Movement (NSM). One of my new high school friends, Margaret Levi, rounded up teen helpers like me for NSM that summer. I pitched in to help rip out walls in an East Baltimore storefront to set up a tutoring center for kids. I continued tutoring with NSM when I went to college in Boston. But my going to a big civil rights demonstration that members of the American Nazi Party said they were planning to attend as well and perhaps disrupt—that made my parents nervous.

Recently, in reading through old 1960s newspapers, I've become more understanding of my parents' fears. It was an uncertain and often violent time. That gives me all the more admiration for those who had the courage of their convictions—and the energy and persistence to keep chipping away at a system that was harsh and unfair, slowly discovering how to force that system to change.

Amy Singewald Nathan
www.AmyNathanBooks.com

Acknowledgments

Warm thanks go to Sharon Langley, one of the first people I interviewed when I started work on this project. How wonderful that as an elementary school educator she is following through on the hope symbolized by her 1963 merry-go-round ride. Special thanks also go to all the others listed in the bibliography who took time from their busy lives to be interviewed.

Others who were very helpful in the research for this book or who made valuable suggestions include: John Gartrell, Baltimore's *Afro-American* newspaper; Francis O'Neill and Marc Thomas, Maryland Historical Society; Courtney Esposito, Becky Haberacker, and Suleyka Lozins, Smithsonian; Stan Hunter and Alemneh Amare, Hunter Concessions; Dr. David T. Terry, Reginald F. Lewis Museum of Maryland African American History and Culture; Bette Largent, National Carousel Association; Doug McElrath and Laura Cleary, University of Maryland's Hornbake Library; Jeff Korman, Enoch Pratt Free Library; Richard Parsons and Jason Domasky, Baltimore County Public Library; Adam Paul, Maryland Transportation Administration; Rev. Dr. John M. Thomas, Madison Avenue Presbyterian Church; Gay-linn Gatewood Jasho, Clark Atlanta University; Michael Bowen Mitchell and Janice Moore, Juanita Jackson Mitchell Multicultural Resource Center; Marion Turner, Walter P. Carter Elementary School; Marc Broady; Jill Carter; Mary Chesnut; Zachary Dixon, Baltimore *Sun* Media Group; Elizabeth Mandeville, Corbis/Bettmann; Matthew Lutts, AP Images; Jay D. Smith and John M. Condon, Hearst Corporation; Zdzislawa Coleman; J.P. Grant; Herbert Harwood; Charly Mann; Trudy Perkins; Linell Smith; Melissa Thompkins; Jacques Kelly; Luyuan Xing; Anne Raver; Susanna Reich; Will Schofield; and Jan and Paul Souza. I'm extremely grateful to the following individuals who took time to read through the manuscript during the review process, offering helpful comments: Vinnie Bagwell, Taylor Branch, John Corenswet, Larry S.

Gibson, Debra Newman Ham, James Henretta, Jean Hess, Beatty Levi, Margaret Levi, Charles Mason, John Roemer, Linell Smith, Dr. David T. Terry, Rabbi Arthur Waskow, Mary Sue Welcome, and Rev. Sheridan T. Yeary.

I am so pleased that James Singewald took photos of the Carousel on the Mall, that the Smithsonian and Hunter Concessions granted permission for the photos to be taken, and that Sarah Keys Evans, Angela Robinson, Karen Carney, Ben Conry, and Mary and Steve Coleman rounded up youngsters to appear in the photos. Special thanks go to the kids who gave up a Saturday morning to be photographed—Jhade and Cameron Carney, Lilah Coleman, and Daniel and Elijah Conry.

In addition, I'd like to thank my brother and sister, Rock Singewald and Tera Younger, for sharing their memories of Gwynn Oak, and my sons Eric and Noah Nathan for their encouragement. I'm grateful to Sarah Keys Evans for helping to guide me in my efforts to write about civil rights, and to Ida Mae Atkinson for giving me my first lessons about the evils of Jim Crow. I'm also glad that Paul Dry, who took a class with me when we were both at Harvard, sent me an e-mail out of the blue two years ago asking if I had any manuscripts that might be of interest to his publishing company. How lucky that he took an interest in this project and prodded me to expand my research.

My parents, Patti and Lou Singewald, lifelong Baltimoreans, would have loved to share Baltimore tales with me for this book. They passed away long before I began this project, but their influence remains strong for having instilled in me a belief in fairness and justice. Of course, there is someone else without whom this book would never have happened: my husband, Carl, an enthusiastic believer right from the start. Thank you, Carl, for constant encouragement, gentle editorial advice, love, and support.

Credits

PHOTO CREDITS

Cover (top, bottom middle), ii (background), 11, 14, 42, 64, 78, 94, 116, 126, 154, 170, 186, 214, 223, 224, 226, back cover: © 2010 James Singewald; Cover (bottom right), ii (foreground), 2, 5, 60 (bottom), 72, 134, 150, 158, 175, 200, 216, 217: Courtesy Baltimore Sun Company, Inc., All Rights Reserved; Cover (bottom left), vi, 31, 32, 57, 67, 68, 97, 99, 113, 120, 161, 162, 168, 180, 184, 189: Courtesy of the Afro-American Newspapers Archives and Research Center; vii, 7: © Bob Adelman/Corbis; 17, 18: Courtesy Baltimore County Public Library, Legacy Web photo collection; 21, 48, 54, 207, 208: Courtesy Library of Congress; 29, 38: Courtesy of Michael Bowen Mitchell and the Juanita Jackson Mitchell Multicultural Resource Center, Roland Park Country School, Baltimore, Maryland; 40: Courtesy Enoch Pratt Free Library, Maryland's State Library Resource Center, Baltimore, Maryland; 44, 80, 82, 104, 121, 123, 142, 144, 159, 178: © Associated Press; 60 (top), 86, 89, 92: © Bettmann/Corbis; 70: © George J. Voith; 75, 108, 109, 118, 132, 135, 149, 163, 195, 203, 205, 210: Courtesy Hearst Corporation, from Special Collections, University of Maryland Libraries; 93: Courtesy Sarah Keys Evans; 105: Courtesy Mary Sue Welcome; 128: Courtesy Jill Carter; 140, 221: © 2010 Amy Nathan; 192 : Courtesy Baltimore Sun Company, Inc., All Rights Reserved/Baltimore Examiner and Washington Examiner; 202: Courtesy Charly Mann.

TEXT CREDITS

Quotes from the writings of Dr. Martin Luther King, Jr., on pages 9, 78, 83, 147, 154, and 197 are reprinted by arrangement with The Heirs of the Estate of Martin Luther King Jr., c/o Writers House as agent for the proprietor, New York, NY. Copyright 1963 Dr. Martin Luther King Jr; copyright renewed 1991 Coretta Scott King. Excerpts from *Baltimore Afro-American* editorials and from articles written by James D. Williams and Mary Sue Welcome are reprinted with the permission of the Afro-American Newspapers Archives and Research Center Archives and Research Center. Excerpts from Oral Histories of Rev. Marion C. Bascom, Juanita Jackson Mitchell, Walter Sondheim, Jr., Robert Watts, and Verda Welcome that were recorded by the Maryland Historical are reprinted courtesy of the Maryland Historical Society. The quote on page 12 from Rev. Marion C. Bascom comes from an Oral History recorded as part of the "Baltimore 68: Riots and Rebirth" project and is printed courtesy of the University of Baltimore, Langsdale Library.

Index

AMY NATHAN is an award-winning author of such books as *Yankee Doodle Gals, Count On Us, Take a Seat—Make a Stand,* and *The Young Musician's Survival Guide.* A Harvard graduate with master's degrees from the Harvard Graduate School of Education and Columbia's Teachers College, she grew up in Baltimore where she went to Western High School.

Visit her at www.AmyNathanBooks.com.